Books by Jorie Graham

HYBRIDS OF PLANTS AND OF GHOSTS

EROSION

THE END OF BEAUTY

REGION OF UNLIKENESS

MATERIALISM

MATERIALISM

MATERIALISM

POEMS BY

JORIE GRAHAM

THE ECCO PRESS

The Ecco Press
100 *West Broad Street, Hopewell, NJ* 08525
Published simultaneously in Canada by Penguin Books Canada Ltd., Ontario
Printed in the United States of America
Designed by Cynthia Krupat
FIRST EDITION

Grateful acknowledgment is made to the editors of the following magazines in which these poems (or
earlier versions of them) first appeared: The New Yorker, Grand Street, The Yale Review, The
Harvard Review, The Threepenny Review, Parnassus, The Wallace Stevens Journal,
and The Paris Review.
Thanks to Connie Brothers, Frank Conroy, Maggie Conroy, Joanna Klink, Mark Strand, Louise
Glück, Frank Bidart, Robert Hass, Stephen Schultz, Rod Zeitler, Alan Gurganus, Jane Miller,
Lynne McMahon and David Skorton . . . Thanks to the John D. and Catherine T. MacArthur
Foundation for a Fellowship which has permitted me some time away from teaching in which to
undertake this work . . . Thanks, too, to Deb West for her indefatigable efforts.

Library of Congress Cataloging-in-Publication Data
Graham, Jorie, 1951-
Materialism : poems / by Jorie Graham. — 1st ed.
p.   cm. — *(American poetry series)*
ISBN 0-88001-342-7
I. *Title.* II. *Series.*
PS3557.R214M38   1993
811'.54—dc20   93-27828
                                                    CIP

The text of this book is set in Electra.

FOR JIM AND EM

(and not without Marilynne)—

AND FOR MY FATHER

CONTENTS

A CAPPELLA

1

We have but one simple method of delivering our sentiments, namely, we must bring men to particulars and their regular series and order, and they must for a while renounce their notions and begin to form an acquaintance with things. . . .

Yet the human understanding resembles not a dry light, but admits a tincture of will and the passions—hence contemplation mostly ceases with sight, and a very scanty or perhaps no regard is paid to invisible objects. . . .

And, too, the human understanding is by its own nature prone to abstraction. It supposes that which is fluctuating to be fixed. But it is better, much better, to dissect than abstract. . . .

(SIR FRANCIS BACON)

2

Well then, added Socrates, let us suppose that there are two sorts of existence—one seen, the other unseen.
Let us suppose then.
The seen is the changing, and the unseen is the unchanging?
That may also be supposed.
And, further, is not one part of us body, another part soul?
To be sure.
And is the soul seen or not seen?
Not seen?
Unseen then?
Unseen.
The soul is more like to the unseen, and the body to the seen?
Yes.
And were we not saying long ago that the soul when using the body as

an instrument of perception—that is to say, when using the sense of sight or hearing or some other sense—were we not saying that the soul too is then dragged by the body into the region of the changeable, and wanders, and is confused—the world spins round her—and she is like a drunkard when she touches change?

(PLATO)

3

And is it not an odd jealousy, that the poet finds himself not ever near enough to his object? The pinetree, the river, the bank of flowers before him—there is always this sense of stillness that follows a pageant which has just gone by; always a referred existence, an absence, never a presence and a satisfaction . . . What shall we say of this flattery and baulking, of this use that is made of us?

(EMERSON)

4

Appearances, now or henceforth, indicate what you are;

Thrive, cities! bright your freight, bring your shows, ample and
    sufficient rivers;
Expand, being; keep your places objects.

We descend upon you and all things—we arrest you all;
We *realize* the soul only by you, you faithful solids and fluids;
Through you color, form, location, sublimity, ideality;
Through you every proof, comparison, and all the suggestions
    and determinations of ourselves.

You have waited, you always wait, you dumb, beautiful ministers!

We receive you with free sense at last, and are insatiate hence-
    forward;
Not you any more shall be able to foil us, or withhold yourselves
    from us;
We use you, and do not cast you aside—we plant you perma-
    nently within us;
We fathom you not—we love you.

(WHITMAN)

5

"Crito, we owe a cock to Asclepios. Pay my debt. Do not forget."

Socrates (PLATO)

MATERIALISM

Watching the river, each handful of it closing over the next,
brown and swollen. Oaklimbs,
gnawed at by waterfilm, lifted, relifted, lapped-at all day in
this dance of non-discovery. All things are
possible. Last year's leaves, coming unstuck from shore,
rippling suddenly again with the illusion,
and carried, twirling, shiny again and fat,
towards the quick throes of another tentative
conclusion, bobbing, circling in little suctions their stiff
                                          presence
on the surface compels. Nothing is virtual.
The long brown throat of it sucking up from some faraway melt.
Expression pouring forth, all content no meaning.
The force of it and the thingness of it identical.
Spit forth, licked up, snapped where the force
exceeds the weight, clickings, pockets.
A long sigh through the land, an exhalation.
I let the dog loose in this stretch. Crocus
appear in the gassy dank leaves. Many
earth gasses, rot gasses.
I take them in, breath at a time. I put my
breath back out
onto the scented immaterial. How the invisible
roils. I see it from here and then
I see it from here. Is there a new way of looking—
valences and little hooks—inevitabilities, proba-
bilities? It flaps and slaps. Is this body the one
I know as me? How private these words? And these? Can you
smell it, brown with little froths at the rot's lips,
meanwhiles and meanwhiles thawing then growing soggy then
the filaments where leaf-matter accrued round a
pattern, a law, slipping off, precariously, bit by bit,

and flicks, and swiftnesses suddenly more water than not.
The nature of goodness the mind exhales.
I see myself. I am a widening angle of
and *nevertheless* and *this performance has rapidly*—
nailing each point and then each next right point, inter-
locking, correct, correct again, each rightness snapping loose,
floating, hook in the air, swirling, seed-down,
quick—*the evidence of the visual henceforth*—and henceforth, loosening—

In the rear-view mirror I saw the veil of leaves
suctioned up by a change in current
and how they stayed up, for the allotted time,
in absolute fidelity to the force behind,
magenta, hovering, a thing that happens,
slowly upswirling above the driveway
I was preparing to back clear out of—
and three young pine trees at the end of that view
as if aghast with bristling stillness—
and the soft red updraft without hesitation
aswirl in their prickly enclosing midst—
and on the radio I bent to press on,
a section with rising strings plugging in,
crisp with distinctions, of the earlier order.
Oh but I haven't gotten it right.
You couldn't say that it was matter.
I couldn't say that it was sadness.
Then a hat from someone down the block
blown off, rolling—tossing—across the empty macadam,
an open mouth, with no face round it,
O and O and O and O—
"we have to regain the moral pleasure
of experiencing the distance between subject and object,"
—me now slowly backing up
the dusty driveway into the law
composed of updraft, downdraft, weight of these dried
                                    mid-winter leaves,
light figured-in too, I'm sure, the weight of light,
and angle of vision, dust, gravity, solitude,
and the part of the law which is the world's waiting,
and the part of the law which is my waiting,

and then the part which is my impatience—now; *now?*—

though there are, there really are,
things in the world, you must believe me.

1) start in the middle and 2) be self-
effacing said the voice—remote and merciful it seemed—
in the dream and then I woke.
Daylight was already trying out eloquence.
Out the window the tin roofs twitched.
Ping ping went the ribs of them, shrill scansion.
The day unfolding its stern materialism. Right down
to the ant-hills. The fingerprints. The pollen frothing
the edges of the rain-filled cavities.
A silver dog-dish? Declivity in the kingdom of the side-
walk? Filigree and harrow gorged with
difference—here blur of slick grasses, there
scribble of early-spring oak-ropes the sudden rain
                              dragged down,
and seven varnished mailboxes in full sun,
and web-silk between them,
and (hearing it now) (inside) the clock-dial hum—
feelers navigating the 12 acid-green islands
over and over. . . . Things
                    detached from us. Immaculate. Good.
Not to be part says the sun.
Not to be says the thunder gone from us now but not
                              so far.
A morning deluge and then this blue.
A feeling, in the living, of a *form*—what has passed.
Like a clarity that has slipped away leaving its outline
in the mind. Remote. Something we shared, each in our
room. Described when we weren't listening.
The author gone. But here, twinkling among us, this applause
and tiny breezy winds, mittened, scribbling.
The children having grown and gone.
The waves of things upon us

having become . . .
Wingless, is it—*I, I*—
this thing that resumes, awakening?
And look how the light puts on its cellophane!
Do I begin? Do I re-enter something now?
Here you are it seems to susurrate, gossipy with
my arrival, pulsating as my glance—surveyor of edges—
                                        descends.
First this. *Then* this . . . Oh, glance—gnawing the
                                        overgrowth,
criss-crossing the open for broken spots, leaks—
what is there? what is
the object? Look: see the face without eyes. Don't be
afraid—twitch, lisp, slur—scuffling
in the dried leaves—grease where the magnet
was supposed to snag—rapture—clubbed rootings the
clay earth won't take—ventriloquial breeze on which the
furry gypsy-moths from the immensities of x
now constellate. Look and look. There is nothing to
feel—tick tock—there is no end of thought, no final
                                        place
where we sit down, as on this bed here now, right on the
                                        tasseled edge,
and take a breath, and count up what we have, what we
                                        have had—
It was like . . . like . . .
it was like something that I thought—
And then the key the hand retrieves from the bedside
                                        table—
such strength there at the tips of fingers in
the human hand—and then the keyhole it's slipped into,
                        the palm that closes up on it—

and then the narrow reddish-papered corridor
the body of the visitor
must feed.

NOTES ON THE REALITY OF THE SELF

In my bushes facing the bandpractice field,
in the last light, surrounded by drumbeats, drumrolls,
there is a wind that tips the reddish leaves
exactly all one way, seizing them up from underneath, making them
barbarous in unison. Meanwhile the light insists they glow
where the wind churns, or, no, there is a wide gold corridor
of thick insistent light, layered with golds, as if runged,
as if laid low from the edge of the sky,
in and out of which the coupling and uncoupling
limbs—the racks of limbs—the luminosities of branchings—
offspring and more offspring—roil—(except when a sudden
                                        stillness reveals
an appal of pure form, pure light—
every rim clear, every leaf serrated, tongued—stripped
of the gauzy quicknesses which seemed its flesh)—but then
                                        the instabilities
regroup, and the upper limbs of the tall oaks
begin to whine again with wide slappings
which seep ever-downward to my bushes—into them, through them—
to where the very grass makes congress with the busyness—
mutating, ridging, threshing this light from that, to no
avail—and in it all
the drumroll, rising as the ranks join in,
the wild branches letting the even drumbeats through,
ripples let through as the red branches spiral, tease,
as the crescendos of the single master-drummer
rise, and birds scatter over the field, and the wind makes each
                                        thing
kneel and rise, kneel and rise, never-ending stringy
almost maternal lurching of wind
pushing into and out of the russets, magentas, incarnadines . . .
Tell me, where are the drumbeats which fully load and expand
                                        each second,

bloating it up, cell-like, making it real, where are they
to go, what will *they* fill up
pouring forth, pouring round the subaqueous magenta bushes
which dagger the wind back down on itself,
tenderly, prudently, almost loaded down
with regret? For there is not a sound the bushes will take
from the multitude beyond them, in the field, uniformed—
(all left now on one heel) (right) (all fifty trumpets up
to the sun)—not a molecule of sound
from the tactics of this glistening beast,
forelimbs of silver (trombones, french horns)
(annointed by the day itself) expanding, retracting,
bits of red from the surrounding foliage deep
                in all the fulgid
instruments—orient—ablaze where the sound is released—
trumpeting, unfolding—
                     screeching, rolling, patterning, measuring—
scintillant beast the bushes do not know exists
as the wind beats them, beats in them, beats round them,
them in a wind that does not really even now
                        exist,
in which these knobby reddish limbs that do not sway
                by so much as an inch
its arctic course
                themselves now sway—

In the bakeshop, at one of the tables,
there is a man about to eat his morning's slice,
who sits, hands folded eyes closed,
above the loaf still entire, and speaks inwardly
huge strange thoughts of thanks.
The knife, a felled birch left overnight
for tomorrow's work on which the moonlight,
in the eyes of no one, plays, gleaming, the knife
sits awaiting the emptiness it will make appear
where all along there had been emptiness
implied. Round him the room hums
slightly. No. Round him
infinite spaces gnaw at his face.
His hands are thick from work. The small hairs
glow—the fresh-washed skin, freckled a bit
with age, ripples where his fingers
lace. His weight is on his elbows, and carries through
onto the imitation-woodgrain tabletop.
Nothing distracts. The loaf is a crucial landmark
in the small landscape which is his place—
a way to find the road back to the felled
tree, even in moonlight, even if strong rains intervene
and no moon or sunshine can get through. For days
he hunted for the tree. Found it. Now
mist makes the most familiar turns implausible,
and notches in skyline, timberline—friends,
guides—suddenly silt in. Silence of a place
known forever then not known at all—never at all.
Habit gone, yesterday and yesterday and yesterday . . .
                                                  Beauty
is the notch restored,
the clump of evergreens—beneath it—recognized!—

three redbirds in them and then two now, up and out, chasing the
                                                            third,
bursting the air all round like water when the monster's
surfacing. All this is true. All this is huge and empty
spaces, tapping his lids, his hands,
legend, small whirling motes
or sparks or seed, inside the hollows—ears, palms—inside the skull,
hands to his lips so briefly as he finishes—a kiss.
Oh glance, now that the eyes that own you open again,
hand, moving out to lift the knife—what
are you doing? Corridor, stairway, front door—

CONCERNING THE RIGHT TO LIFE

1

As I rounded the corner—noiselessly—as if wide unseeable
        doors slid open—*intelligent*—almost a halo with
hinges—almost a split where something
        overripens—
I came upon the rose
        tall as a man
on its senseless stem,
        thorns like equal-signs all the way up—
each tip looking as if the air were cut

        open right there by its
idea—
        all round it the invisible
scent,
        rough muscle,
drenched veil—As I
        rounded the corner, the possible
sprung from
        possibility

        into whipped red
choice.
        I looked into its face—its authorship—accretion of
discardings
        all whispering at once—
looked for the *living* in there—half-awake—
        sultry, a fellow destiny to mine—
courage here not the issue

        or what is *good*—

only the form that
matters—
how at the core, at the end, there is
a thrashing forking red, and how
around it—shuddering—the invisible
ripens, parent . . .
I touched it.   My fate

crossed out along my silly white extended arm—five

fingers flared
to somehow prolong desire
out past the sticky glove of
matter—Touched

its lip—thin and resilient as my sleeping child's,
barely trembling—Stopped
and tried to look at it—
A long distance—

my shadow from the time of day upon it—
on Tuesday—
remembering then those locked in the cattlecars—
remembering them with my hand as I run my finger on the tip—

those waving goodbye as the doors close—
The shutting doors sliding loomlike
across the stiff even rows of faces—

and then this one face in the dusk my hand upon it—
Pity us, dusk light—
Judge us, red rose—do not let us pass unjudged—

2

The clinic's layers of glass door glide open.   Tiny hiss.

    Outside the protest continues—

from inside a muffling
    sound, making us feel, in the waiting room,
ourselves unborn. . . .

    I try to feel it, beneath my
magazine,
    the immaculate spot within—the freedom of
choice, illustrious
    sleep, bloody spot. . . .
                    Now I lay me
    down to

sleep—tick tock—I pray thee Lord
    to make these words have
materiality—
    make there be a tiny draft
just underneath them—there—make them displace something to
    be—something that opens—sliding

back—firm
    over the fault—a *subject*—indifferent to rot as matter,
                        rotting, is
indifferent. . . . Out there (framed by the gleaming levelors) some
    voices screaming *right to life*, some others screaming
choice choice—

    placards above bodies—an old man

(suit and tie) screaming *pseudo-christians* at the photos of
fetuses blossoming
       bloody
at the tops of their stems—one nun

staring out
       at some orphaned perfection undressed before her—
above her (in magic-marker): *the other*
       holocaust: don't kill
your children—
       all round her the bodies lying down (it's
crowded), the young policeman's

       shy angelic face, his glittering new
uniform—
       (*home* behind him, *home* before him)
(and the immanence of day)
       leaves blowing across as

       one girl's red dress
wraps suddenly round her—terra
       infidel—(if only we could rid ourselves
of pity)—acacias on fire in
       the parking lot—

"let the mother die but save the child"
the huge man screams—
                              as the
siren—
       its one intransigent mythology, high-pitched,
clean as a knife—(oh glitzy splendor of the shiny *me*)—
       kicks in—

What can happen?
    What is the worst that can happen?

3

The storm has struck, the weather channel says
    the worst has passed.
I sponge your sleeping brow—
    trying not to wake your
pain again—104 and holding—when does the
    medicine kick in?—I want
your blood to cool, my blood is shrieking that your
    blood, there on its path inside, *must cool*—
Cicadas will begin again now that the storm
    has done—it will be

    normal—we will
fore-
    see
tomorrow and tomorrow and tomorrow's
    weather—I read the label on the medicine.
How many hours have passed (I count again)—
    It seems the shadows of your room
ring round—*there is no choice*—and yet your yellow
    lion winks, your horse leans
softly to the wall—

your 3 *1st prizes* (on the shelf)—
    a note you got from a *best friend*—

It is a mountain. And then it is a sea.

4

What is it, the spot inside Mary, the punched-out spot of
blood which is *not her?*—
    to whom does it belong?—immaculate
garden—red idea; truth held *self-*
        evident—
through which the crowd can cross

    and *take possession*
of the earth—
    So she is a shore, a *vulgar ocean* which round the *idea of*
                                        ocean
roils—

5

    . . . for I see a thousand kinds of trees (Tuesday October 23)
each of which has its own kind of fruit (1492)
    and they are green now as in Spain in the month of
May and June
    and the same with flower and with
everything—but that I do not
    recognize them
burdens me with the greatest sorrow

in the world—
    nothing was recognized,
nothing!—
    except the red aloe
of which today I have ordered great quantities
    brought to the ship

to take to Your
    Highness—

and it is raining a lot
    and yesterday it rained a lot without being cold—
rather the day is hot and the nights temperate
    as in May in Spain in Andalusia. . . .

from Sir Francis Bacon's NOVUM ORGANUM

(AN ADAPTATION)

Let the first motion be that of the resistance of matter, which exists in every particle, and completely prevents its annihilation; so that no conflagration, weight, pressure, violence, or length of time can reduce even the smallest portion of matter to nothing, or prevent it from being something, and occupying some space, and delivering itself (whatever straits it be put to), by changing its form or place, or, if that be impossible, remaining as it is; nor can it ever happen that it should either be nothing or nowhere.

Let the second motion be that which we term the motion of connection, by which bodies do not allow themselves to be separated at any point from the contact of another body, delighting, as it were, in the mutual connection and contact. This is called by the schools a motion to prevent a vacuum. It takes place when water is drawn up by suction or a syringe, the flesh by cupping, or when the water remains without escaping from perforated jars, unless the mouth be opened to admit the air—and innumerable instances of a like nature.

Let the third be that which we term the motion of liberty, by which bodies strive to deliver themselves from any unnatural pressure or tension, and to restore themselves to the dimensions suited to their mass.

Let the fourth be that which we term the motion of matter, and which is opposed to the last; for in the motion of liberty, bodies abhor, reject, and avoid a new size or volume, or any new expansion or contraction (for these different terms have the same meaning), and strive, with all their power, to rebound and resume their former density; on the contrary, in the motion of matter, they are anxious to acquire a new volume or dimension, and attempt it willingly and rapidly, and occasionally by a most vigorous effort, as in the example of gunpowder.

Let the fifth be that which we term the motion of continuity. We do not understand by this simple and primary continuity with any other body (for that is the motion of connection), but the continuity of a particular body in itself; for it is most certain that all bodies abhor a solution of continuity, some more and some less, but all partially.

Let the sixth be that which we term the motion of acquisition, or the motion of need. It is that by which bodies placed amongst others of a heterogeneous and, as it were, hostile nature, if they meet with the means or opportunity of avoiding them, and uniting themselves with others of a more analogous nature, even when these latter are not closely allied to them, immediately seize and, as it were, select them, and appear to consider it as something acquired (whence we derive the name), and to have need of these latter bodies. For instance, gold, or any other metal in leaf, does not like the neighborhood of air; if, therefore, they meet with any tangible and thick substance (such as the finger, paper, or the like) they immediately adhere to it, and are not easily torn from it. Paper, too, and cloth, and the like, do not agree with the air, which is inherent and mixed in their pores. They readily, therefore, imbibe water or other liquids, and get rid of the air. Sugar, or a sponge, dipped in water or wine, and though part of it be out of the water or wine, and at some height above it, will yet gradually absorb them.

Let the seventh be that which we term the motion of greater congregation, by which bodies are borne towards masses of a similar nature, for instance, heavy bodies towards the earth, light to the sphere of heaven.

Let the eighth be that which we term the motion of lesser congregation, by which the homogeneous parts in any body separate themselves from the heterogeneous and unite together, and whole bodies of a similar substance coalesce and tend towards each other, and are sometimes congregated, attracted, and meet, from some distance.

Let the ninth be the magnetic motion, which, although of the nature of that last mentioned, yet, when operating at great distances, and on great masses, deserves a separate inquiry.

Let the tenth motion be that of avoidance, or that which is opposed to the motion of lesser congregation, by which bodies, with a kind of antipathy, avoid and disperse, and separate themselves from, or refuse to unite themselves with others.

Let the eleventh motion be that of assimilation, or self-multiplication, or simple generation.

Let the twelfth motion be that of excitement.

Let the thirteenth motion be that of impression, which is also a species of motion of assimilation, and the most subtile of diffusive motions.

Let the fourteenth motion be that of configuration or position, by which bodies appear to desire a peculiar situation, collocation, and configuration with others, rather than union or separation. This is a very abstruse notion and has not been well investigated.

Let the fifteenth motion be that of transmission or of passage, by which the powers of bodies are more or less impeded or advanced by the medium, according to the nature of the bodies and their effective powers, and also according to that of the medium. For one medium is adapted to light, another to sound, another to heat and cold, another to magnetic action, and so on. . . .

Let the sixteenth be that which we term the royal or political motion, by which the predominant and governing parts of any body check, subdue, reduce, and regulate the others, and force them to unite, separate, stand still, move, or assume a certain position, not from any inclination of their own, but according to a certain order, and as best suits the convenience of the governing part, so that there is a sort of dominion and civil government exercised by the ruling part over its subjects.

Let the seventeenth position be the spontaneous motion of revolution.

Let the eighteenth motion be that of trepidation.

It is the motion of an (as it were) eternal captivity.

When bodies, for instance, being placed not altogether according to their nature, constantly tremble, and are restless, not contented with their position.

Such is the motion of the heart and pulse of animals.

And it must necessarily occur in all bodies which are situated in a mean state, between convenience and inconvenience.

So that being removed from their proper position, they strive to escape, are repulsed, and again continue to make the attempt. . . .

SUBJECTIVITY

1

Black bars expanding
  over an atomic-yellow ground—feelers retracted—
the monarch lay flat on the street
  and did not move at all
when I lifted it
  onto my spiral
notebook

  and did not move the whole length of the block
during which I held the purple laminated

cover still as
  possible—
my gaze
  vexing the edges of
the wings, ruffling the surface where it seemed
  light from another century
beat against those black bars—yellow, yellow, gorgeous, in-
            candescent—

  bells, chimes, flutes, strings—wind seized and blown
open—butter yellow, fever yellow,
  yellow of acid and flax,
lemon and chrome,
  madder, mikado, justic, canary—

yellow the singers exhale that rises, fanged, laughing,
  up through the architraves and out (slow) through the hard
               web
the rose-windows press
  onto the rising gaze,

5

yellow of cries forced through that mind's design,
    like a clean verdict,
like a structure of tenses and persons for the gusting

    heaven-yellow
minutes (so many flecks, spores,
    in the wide still beam
of sun)
    or the gaze's stringy grid of nerves
spreading out onto

    whatever bright new world the eyes would seize upon—
pronged optic animal the incandescent *thing*
    must rise up to and spread into, and almost burn
                    its way
clear through
    to be.

2

    She sits on the straightback chair in the room.
A ray of sun is calling across the slatwood floor.
    I say *she* because my body is so still
in the folds of daylight
    through which the one beam slants.
I say *calling* because it lays itself down
    with a twang and a licking monosyllable

across the pine floor-boards—
    making a meaning like a wide sharp thought—
an unrobed thing we can see the inside of—
    less place than time—

less time than the shedding skin of time, the thought
                                                of time,

the yellow swath it cuts
        on the continuum—
now to the continuum
        what she is to me,
a ceremonial form, an intransigent puissant corridor
                                nothing will intersect,

and yet nothing really
        —dust, a little heat . . .
She waits.
        Her leg extended, she waits for it—
foot, instep, calf—
        the I, the beam
of sun—
        the *now* and *now*—

it moving like a destiny across,
        neither lured-on nor pushed-forward,
without architecture,
        without
beginning,
        over the book lying in the dust,

over the cracked plank—down into the crack—across—

not animal,
        nothing that can be deduced-from or built-upon,
aswarm with dust and yet
        not entered by the dust,

27

not *touched*—
    smearing everything with a small warm gaiety—

over the pillow-seam over the water glass—

    cracking and bending but not cracking or bending—

over the instep now, holding the foot—

    her waiting to feel the warmth then beginning
to feel it—
    the motion of it and the warmth of it not identical—
the one-way-motion of it, the slow sweep,
    approaching her as a fate approaches, inhuman but
                           resembling
feeling,

without deviation,
    turning each instant a notch deeper towards
the only forwards,
    but without beginning,
and never—not ever—
    not moving
forwards . . .

Meanwhile the knowledge of things lies round,
    over which the beam—
Meanwhile the transparent air
    through or into which the beam—
over the virtual and the material—
    over the world and over the world of the beholder—
glides:

it does not change, crawler, but things are
changed—
    the mantle, the cotton-denim bunched at
                        the knees—

diamonds appearing on the tips of things then disappearing—
    each edge voluble with the plushnesses of silence—

    now up to her folded arms—warm under the elbow—
almost a sad smell in the honeyed yellow—
    (the ridge of the collarbone) (the tuck of the neck)
till suddenly (as if by
    accident)

    she is inside—(ear, cheek)—the slice of time

now on the chin, now on
    the lips, making her rise up into me,
forcing me to close my eyes,
    the whole of the rest feeling broken off,

it all being my face, my being inside the beam of sun,

    and the sensation of how it falls unevenly,

    how the wholeness I felt in the shadow is lifted,
broken, this tip *lit*, this other *dark*—and stratified,
    analysed, chosen-round, formed—

3

    Home I slid it gently
into the book,

wings towards the center of the
page,
    the body denser and harder to press
flat,
    my mind hovering over it,
huge, ballooning, fluttering, yellow,
      and back and forth,
and searching for the heaviest book
      to lay upon
the specimen,
    to make it flat—

    as if it were still too plural, too
shade-giving, where the mind needs it
      so flat the light can't
round it, licking for crevices, im-
                perfections,

even the wings still arced enough to bring
                awake
    the secret blacknesses
of the page—
    bits of shadow off the feelers, soft dry bits off
                the tiny
head—
    like a betrothal of the thing to the world—
a chattery, quivery moulting of

    the thing—body and wings—
so that each way I slide it the shadows slide—
    almost a green in their grey—
everything on the verge—
    the edge of the trunk furry—

the ever-so-slightly serrated rim of the wing—
    everywhere the soft grey exaggeration—
below, around—
    as if leaking from some *underneath*—

so that it is the *underneath* the mind wants to eliminate—
    the imitation? the interpretation?—
me carrying, through the bountiful morning-light, the dictionaries in—
    and the 2 inches of body and 5 inches of wing dripping with these
yellowish glances,
    these thin almost icy beams I can feel my open eyes release,
widening as they sweep down
    out of the retina

    to take the body in—
aerial, tunneling, wanting to be spent in what cannot
    feel them as they smear, coat,
wrap, diagram—

    from next door C stopping to bring the lilies in—
that butterfly's not dead, you know, she adds
    noticing,
cold mornings like these they're very still—see (gliding it onto
                                    the broad-leaved stem)
    put it in sun (walking back out),
the day like a tunnel she's in,
    the yellow thing at the end of her stalk and then,
placed on the lawn,
    the yellow thing, the specimen,
rising up of a sudden out of its envelope of glances—

a bit of fact in the light and then just light.

2.026   There must be objects, if the world is to have an unalterable form.

2.027   Objects, the unalterable, and the subsistent are one and the same.

2.0271   Objects are what is unalterable and subsistent; their configuration is what is changing and unstable.

2.0272   The configuration of objects produces states of affairs.

2.03   In a state of affairs objects fit into one another like the links of a chain.

2.031   In a state of affairs objects stand in a determinate relation to one another.

2.032   The determinate way in which objects are connected in a state of affairs is the structure of the state of affairs.

2.033   Form is the possibility of structure.

2.034   The structure of a fact consists of the structures of states of affairs.

2.04   The totality of existing states of affairs is the world.

2.05   The totality of existing states of affairs also determines which states of affairs do not exist.

2.06   The existence and non-existence of states of affairs is reality. (We also call the existence of states of affairs a positive fact, and their non-existence a negative fact.)

2.061   States of affairs are independent of one another.

2.062   From the existence or non-existence of one state of affairs it
             is impossible to infer the existence or non-existence of another.

2.063   The sum-total of reality is the world.

RELATIVITY: A QUARTET

1

During the slowdown we lost power
    along the northeast corridor—it taking a moment before I
                      realized
we were at a crawl, then the slow
        catch,
    and we were still. I heard the cars behind me each
receive the jolt
    of stillness.
Felt the transfer of

inertia
    slither through,
creaking,
    then an aftershock—
long the backbone.
    Nothing shrill. A hiss clenched it.

    Across the aisle a girl and her father woke, looked out.
Monologue of going and going interrupted.
    The land looked truant, incomplete. On their side, through
                      trees,
the ocean looked too pressed with
    definition? incomparability? what is it that leaks
            out of it, *scene,*
once it's the untheoretical *here*—sylvan, yes, but almost
    dishonored by mere,

still, being? On my side, leaves against the
    glass and then, left frame, on the rooftop of some walled industrial
                    facility,

a mounted, scanning, video-cam—
    searching for what?—inside the walls then out—
(no windows there)—(below, a parking lot)—
    lens all one way, then back the
other way . . . *Where is*, I think,

    watching again,
the blind spot in its turn?
    Across the aisle (now lights are out) the sea's skin
gleams.
    Two clouds. Two evergreens.
My neighbors have gone back to sleep.
    When does it change—the frame around her scene,

the frame around my scene?
    After a while I see he's not her dad.
Then that they're stoned and cannot help the sleep.
    The sea that holds them in its frame—stuck there—
itself is stuck, slick gaping eyelessness.
    Where is the news account?
Where is the *varnished* sea? where the ventriloquial sea, the fast
                              train—panning

glints—scribble of shifting points of view—
    wave-tips frothing as the eye
blinks and the venue slips
    to the new sea—*of faces*, say, *of houses*—and then some
                              even newer
sea—hiding its monster? white-eyed? . . . I want it to be again
                    what it was—
    to go by and go by, as if matter itself were going

on and on to its own
        destination, bouquet of instances collecting all
the swift and cunning and mercenary
        appearances—swish—so that it's *there, there,*
and we can, swaying slightly,
        eyes still, eyes absolutely open receptive and still,
let it lay itself down frame by frame onto the wide
        resistenceless opening of our wet
retina—more and more—
        all the debris, all the astonishments, quicker than single file,
smearing onto us—undestined, undestinied—
        But it is still.   It does not move.

2

Against my pane,
        flat leaves that would bury themselves
into the molecules of glass—pressed
        right up to my eye—(so close they blur)—
the flat cold lingering
        against my skin

        as I pull back.
A scribble of . . . Lowly . . . Green ribbon. They twitch (no
        wind). They peck a bit (now wind). A stratagem
                                        for genuine
utterance—cunning, teasing the invisible tender-minded
                                        spectrum
        of. . . . The cam keeps saying something about

sight—
        about the guaranteed freshness of the world repeating
                                        itself

without meaning—leaf, leaf—
     Shanavasa asked Ananda,
"what is the fundamental uncreated essence of all
          things?"
Come back come back with empty hands, he said,
     and
where can dust collect?
          (*time and again wipe it diligently*)
and
          there has never been anything

given to another, there has never been anything
          received from another . . .
Look close, I think. Stem, node,
          bract, pedicel.
I count the greens.
          I slow along the veins.
And shadow: how it slithers long the rib: how it is seized,

fretted—shouldered here and slipped-off there—
          so that no two faces
match,
          each branch a sea of
individual
          tremblings—
I want to see through—my window does not open or

          I'd take a leaf—from here
(against the light) the chlorophyll exists inside the plasts
          and (where sun is strongest) light
thickens
          drawing the carbon
in . . .

Oxygen steams off.
Sun picks up mist.
    Under the face of it I see the pores
between the veins.
    Where the carbon molecule must pass. Where the hydrogen
                         molecule
must pass.
    Inside, inside.
Envelope, rib, protein, thylakoid,
    starch grain,
acid strand.

And the cuticle of the leaf brim.
    And the loosely packed layer of photosynthetic tissue,
guard cells,
    substomatal chambers. . . .

    I blink.   I don't *see anything.*
Lord,
    I want to see this leaf. I'd shut my hand all round it. I'd press it,
                          tight.

3

    What does she have, my twin, the sleeper, there, unseized,
in her window-sea?
    God's adversary: the waters?
Unfanged, unhanded, unlimbed, unheaded?
    Hooves and hooves and hooves and hooves?
The protozoa bloom all over its back.
    It hunches and slacks. Amasses and slacks.
All its passageways gleam.
    They breathe, the two of them.

They have a shopping bag on the floor between them—a large
                                        toy train

        in glistening packaging—red white and blue
and green and chrome.
        Thou didst divide the sea by thy strength: thou breakest
the heads of the dragons
        in the waters:
thou driest up the mighty river:
        the day is thine:
thou hast prepared the light:
        thou hast set all the borders of:
when the waves of the sea arise
        thou stillest them:
with thy strong arm:
        awake awake:
awake awake:
        thou hast made over the deep of the sea a way
for the ransomed to pass over—

        Green leaves: cloth to shroud the Deep:
ride above the deep:
        ride in your chariot of shapeliness:
clean: shut: not this and not this:
        destroy with one seed the monster's skull:
thrust with one stem a sword into its heart—

        And the waters fled *backwards*—
And the endlessness fearfully surrendered—
        And the branching dried up the floods,
dividing,
        dividing,

and the minutes sang, each to each,
    and the minutes the sons of god shouted for joy, tick tock,

    thus the work of creation was
completed.
    And I see on her arms the needle tracks.
His neck—long where it's tossed in sleep—has tracks.
    And the tops of her hands, folded, tracked.
She's wearing running shoes.   She's shivering—

    asleep and shivering. Wouldn't you cover her
with the man-sized coat bunched up beside her,
    just take it gently—(like this)—holding my breath—
and pull it over her—(like this)—(as if to hide her)—
    but she will waken suddenly
and think I'm stealing it
    and scream
and will not listen where I'm trying to
    explain.
She hits my face.
    Making my right eye smart.
It's like a dream but it is not a dream.

4

What would you cover up?
    what, recover from His sight?
What, restore to the deep
    sleep and
why? *Whir.*
    We have been monitoring developments.
The first shells fell just a 100 yards from.
    Others were killed on the way to.

As the search for food becomes more difficult.
    Lost his legs on the way to.
Earlier the representative said.
    The People's Congress said.
The prime minister said.
    Lost his legs in the attack, up the front steps.

    Others were killed on the way to;
others were killed on the way too;
    and in a border-skirmish at dawn the parties involved pledged—
What is the fundamental uncreated essence of all
    things the representative
asked—
    Come back come back with empty hands the minister
pledged—In

    1982 on the downtown Express just out of 72nd Street,
having found a seat in what is like a dream, the sideways-rocking
    mixed-in with the forward
lunge making me slightly
    sleepy, watching the string of white faces lined up across from
                                            me—
the interlocking vertebrae
    of the endless twisting creature's spine—

    watching it lob to absorb the shocks—
watching it twist all one way to wreathe
    the rudderless turns—
watching the eyes in it narrow, widen, as the tunnelling forwardness
    cleaved to its waiting like flesh—
widen and narrow—blinking—the whole length of the train (I thought)
    this dynamism of complex acceptance,
sleepy, staring out,

blinking, some equation getting counted
out—change by change—sometimes the elbows touching, sometimes
        the seam at
  the thigh—plus or minus—some long bit of
thought—what needs to be under-
  gone that the solution be

found—sleepy—then
  an utterly single sound, sawtoothed, a fragment
of some vacuum, flew
  into the car and the woman beside me doubled
over and faster and faster the figures in the long
  equation began to twist and stand—a long distorted
sound—then a snapping into the present tense
  like surfacing and M grabbed me and pushed me
down, *down* he shrieked, and shoved me behind
  the last row of seats and the boy

waving the gun made a shape in the air above his head
  like a wave breaking upon a rock—
or was he giving up?—a shape in the invisible which expresses
  hope, then down came the arm again, and more
shots, and screams, the boy bending forward with his long
  extended arm as if

  trying to include something in himself,
as if trying to sharpen himself for entry,
  the room a brightly-lit hole hurtling through space at 90 mph,
a hole with screams and lights and bullets travelling round,
  holding the emptiness together—so that
it matters—
  light and blood swirling—us down here

on our knees in
	secret, living, living,
my portion of time,
	my portion, full,
(can you stand it?)
	(get down and hide)
(live fast, cloth over a sea, breathe, breathe)

	and at the heart of the living hole the boy, acid,
rare, in support of progress,
	looking for what he's missed,
laughing, gun at the end of his arm, over his
	head, swinging back,
tentacular, spitting seed, him the stalk of
	the day, scattering seed, planting it deep—

here and here—into everything he reaches,
	all things can happen,
wave after wave,
	seek and thou shall find,
and yet so unlikely,
	so that one is not sure of having seen—
wet branches? what was I wearing?
	and then much later, like a dream, desolate, things
					being talked about.

from Dante's INFERNO

(Canto XI)

Then on the upper rim of a deep ravine—
a circular ledge of shattered rocks—
we came upon an even crueler drop

and here, given the horrible rising stench
the hole spit forth, took cover
behind the fallen lid of an imposing vault.

On it I saw some words inscribed—
"Pope Anastasius I now own
whom Fontin tempted from the righteous path."

"Let us postpone descending for a while"
—the Master said—"that you grow used
to the sad stench. After a short while

human senses numb. . . ."
To which I ventured, "may we at least then
use this time—that it not simply register as

lost?" "You've read my mind," he said, "my
son. Within these broken stones, these cliffs,
three interlocking shrinking spheres descend,

three rings, like this one we now leave—and all
are full of spirits cursed and damned.
That, later on, the sight of them—the memory of that

sight—suffice and satisfy your mind,
let me explain, that you may understand,
why it is that they are so confined.

Every wickedness that earns the hatred of
the skies involves Injustice. And each
injustice born of fraud, or misused twisted will,
                                        spills over

like a stain from soul to soul.
And as deceit—of all the sins—remains the one most wholly,
most uniquely, man's, it most arouses the God's

ire. Therefore the liars are at the bottom of the pit.
Therefore most pain assails them. . . .
You see, the whole of the first circle holds the violent,

but because violence always sears three persons,
the circle splits and spills and builds again into three rings.
Violence is done to God. Violence is done to one's

own self. And finally, most literally, to one's own
                                        neighbor is
the violence done . . . Let me explain.
Upon your brother, upon his being and upon

his property, death and ruin may be
wrought. Burnings. Extortions. Devastations.
Therefore the first ring holds the homicides

and everyone who wounds by greed
—pillaging, plundering—all of these souls
in various gathered groups now, drifting.

A man or woman may lay violent hand upon
                                        themselves,

upon their person, or their property,
and so, here in the second ring, each one who has deprived
                                        himself

—by violence or by violent self-destructive disregard,
                        by dissipation—
of your world, your flesh—he who has wept
there where he should be joyous—

here in the second circle must and will
repeatedly repent in vain . . .

But against God violence also may be done.
Denying God, barring God access to your heart,
ignoring Nature, ignoring Nature's power, beauty or
                                        truthfulness.

Look down and see—further in yet—the lower ring
and how it seethes with sodomites and usurers and all
                                        the rest
who secretly speak inwardly against the evidence
                        of God.

Finally, upon the one who trusts in him, upon
                        a friend,
as too upon a total stranger—even an enemy—a man
                        may practice
fraud. It stings. A wound upon conscience.

And though upon a stranger fraud breaks the natural bond
of human love (what we call *nature*)—(and you can see
here in the second ring how all these

hypocrites and flatterers and sorcerers and
thieves and panderers have made
their filthy nest)—the trust placed in a *friend*,

broken, breaks both that natural bond
and the created one—the personal, most crucial bond—So that
                                                          it's in
the smallest, narrowest, darkest spot

at the center of the Universe
that every traitor is consumed, eternally.
Those fires will never cease to burn."

And then I asked him, "Master, your speech
clearly describes this chasm and the souls it holds,
but those souls in the bog, down there,

and them whom the wind drives, and them whom the rain
devours, and those down there who scream and curse—that
                                                    bitterness
I hear—why aren't they punished too in this metropolis of
                                              blood and fire?

or is God's anger not upon them?
And if it isn't, why
do they suffer so?"   And he to me,

"Why do your thoughts wander from their
                                    rightful
course? Where else is your mind
wandering? What do you see?
Don't you recall the words with which the
                                    Ethics names

what God's will most abhors:
incontinence, malice and *mad bestiality*—
and how incontinence offends, but is not damned as
                                        mightily?
Think, therefore, consider and imagine,

who those are that suffer punishment up there—
Can't you see clearly why they're separated from
those other acid souls, why the God's vengeance
hammers them less spitefully?"

"Master, you heal as sunlight would
        my troubled vision.
You make the questioning more valuable
—by your response—than having known, or
                        knowing.   But please

go back to where you said how usury
offends the God.   Free that knot up
                        for me."
That's when he said "for one who's listening,

Philosophy, at every turn, points out
how Nature takes her shape from the God's Intellect.
From His Imagination. So in the *Physics* you will find

that Poetry (as far as it can do)
also must follow Nature's swift
command—this Art of yours,

therefore, almost a grand-child of the God, a great
                        grand-child . . .

Because Man must (remember Genesis)
turn to these two—Nature and God—to make

his life, to prosper, reap, to send forth men
upon the earth. . . . The usurer—
because he goes the other way—contradicts Nature

both in her body and her soul
by trying to hoard and then to squander her.
It seems he would extinguish her rather than spend

her gifts . . . But follow me,

for now it pleases me to go,

the patterns of the stars are quivering
                near the horizon now,
the north wind's picking up, and farther on
there is the cliff's edge we must reach

to start down from." . . .

EVENT HORIZON

(For Bei-Dao, June 1989)

    Then I took the red dress out, put it in a basin. Soap.
Brought the kettle out, poured till full.
    Sunlight teetered at the edge of the thousand-faced
bubble,
    sunlight hovered, pregame, in the chasm of the
millisecond,
    played over the ranks,

    grazed at the upturned shield-tips, faces and faces,
then—pop—went in
    as I pressed down—now on my knees—
to get the dumb stain out.
    Two jays watched from the snow-lowered pinebough.
Two still jays in the swelling instant.
    Poured off the brown water. Started over.

Strutting of sun over fencepoles, river.

Strutting of wind over tops of pine.

    There is history—the story of the man carrying his father
                              on his back—
that stairway—
    narrowing helplessly on the way down.
There is the wind trying to enter the aspen tree—
    wind twisting round and round the wrinkling tree for a while,

trying to narrow itself, force an edge to itself,
    the wind only entering to cross on through.
And there is the girl with her dancing red shoes,
    and how she loved them *too much*, beware,
how her dancing took her away to where the wind

     goes, to where the man and his father came from,
that burning place, Imperial, faces among the flames,
     towers (before they fall) like the exposed rays
of some other star
     deep in the earth,
star made of bricks, piled stone, mortar,
     of rocks being carried thousands of miles

by the backs of creatures some of them human,
     star of *work*—things piled on other things—
a blueprint somewhere down there on a scrap of paper,
     an idea down there somewhere in the mind
of the one looking up, squinting, figuring. . . .
     Cloud-cover. Wind. Shade like a

searchlight upping its ante.
     Gloss gone, the day tries harder to be *really*
seen.
     Squirrel-scold. River-glint.
One woodpecker deep on the south side.
     How to see her this foreign girl?
Shadows unwrap.
     Something walks abroad ignoring things.
Anger freights the edges.
     Some promise, some big one,

kept? unkept?
     One jay, high-pitched.
Nearby? Behind?
     Rising, the second rinse done, dress in hand,
I can feel the mind at its hinge,

insane for foothold.
The bawdy jay shrieks.
    The mind feeling sure there is a beneath—a hard place—

behind the spangly news report . . .
    Then the sun back. The gift beribboned again.
The water, as I toss it out, festooned.
    The fake thing—the blessing—splashed over everything,
almost a hiss—.
    Inside, the anchorman's back, the minutes tick by.
The government in Beijing *has cut off all satellite*

    transmission
and all we get is the anchor's face
    and sometimes voice-over onto the freeze-frame
where coverage
    was interrupted.
Mostly we get the face—animated—

something in front, something that can be washed off.
    Before there was a close-up on the faces of the *young troops.*
The camera picked up tears or something glistened.
    The skinny boy screamed into the mike
"we think everything must change."
    A crack has appeared between day and night writes
                                    Bei Dao,

    and *you did not get back at the time we*
appointed.
    The dress flaps on the line.
The clean dress flaps in the underneath.
    Beyond it the river's finery, mottling, silky,

and on it something unearthly—
    there on a spot in the middle of its back,
where the sun hits first and most directly,
    where a person can hardly look,
a little gash on the waterfilm,

    an indentation, almost a cut—a foothold—
where the dizziness seems to be rushing towards form,
    pressing down hard where the river flows, down on that skin,
as if the light needed something it does not have,
    down hard on that one-way motion—hard—no turning back—
(how can the water rise up out of its grave of matter?)—
    (how can the light drop down out of its grave of thought?)—

everything at the edges of everything else now rubbing—

    (making tiny sounds that sound like laughter)—

summer, noon, hummings, clicks,
    water currents, arcs of flight,
degrees of temperature and notes, notes,
    the mind, the anchor,
the number of bodies,
    what sounds like gunfire on the blank
screen,
    and the laughter which you might *think* an angel—

    the wind whispering take it or leave it—
the river narrowing, narrowing—
    and the son putting his father down saying here we
are, look around,
    and all around the *above* screaming inaudibly to the *below*:

you did not get back at the time we appointed—
   you did not get back at the time we appointed—
and out there, floating, on the emptiness,

      among the folds of radio signals, hovering, translucent,
inside the dress of fizzing, clicking golden
      frequencies—the pale, invisible flames—
is the face of the most beautiful woman in the world
      at the top of a tower at the heart of these flames

—her living face a stain on the flames—
      and a smile on her face as the hair starts to burn—
the last thing to go that smile at us
      as the face disappears feeding out into

our gaze on her, our long thin gaze,

      then the space where the face has gone and the gaze remains,
pushing out, still probing, nervous,
      the orphaned gaze still sloshing out
onto the smoky upslanting void—
      no image there and the gaze remains—
no place there and the gaze remains—

      and the dress remains, and the flapping thrumming dress all
sleeves of wind
      remains—

ON DESCRIPTION

(from Walter Benjamin's ILLUMINATIONS, *and a letter)*

1

An angel is looking as though he is about to move away from something he is fixedly contemplating. His eyes are staring, his mouth is open, his wings are spread. This is how the angel of history must look. His face is turned toward the past. Where we perceive a chain of events, he sees one single catastrophe that keeps piling wreckage on wreckage and hurls it in front of his feet. The angel would like to stay, awaken the dead, and make whole what has been smashed. But a storm is blowing from Paradise; it has got caught in his wings with such violence that the angel can no longer close them. This storm irresistibly propels him into the future to which his back is turned, while the pile of debris before him grows skyward. This storm is what we call progress.

2

The angel, however, resembles all from which I have had to part: persons and above all *things*. In the things I no longer have, he resides. He makes them transparent, and behind all of them there appears to me the one for whom they are intended. . . .

3

Just as I, no sooner than I had seen you, journeyed back with you, from whence I came.

IN THE HOTEL

(3:17 a.m.)

Whir. The invisible sponsored again by white
walls—a joining in them and then (dark spot)
(like the start of a thought)
a corner, fertilized by shadow, hooked, dotted,
here demurring, there—up there—
almost hot with black. . . . What time is it?
The annihilation. The chaste middle of things.
Then I hear them, whoever they are, as if
inside my wall, as if there were a multitude of tiny wings
                                        trapped
inside the studs and joints.
The clockdial hums.   Greenish glow and twelve stark dots
round which this supple, sinewed, blackest flesh
must roil—vertebrate.   A moaning now—a human moan—and then
another cry—but small—
furry in the way the wall can hold it—no
regret—a cry like a hypothesis—another
cry—the first again?—but not as in
dialogue—no—no question in it,
no having heard—now both—no moods in that room—
no fate—cries the precipitate of something on the verge of—
all of it supple now, threadbare in this black we share,
little whelps, vanquishings, discoveries, here under this
                                        rock,
no, over here, inside this sky, or is it below?—paupers,
                                        spoors—
a common grave—the backbone still glowing green—
and blackness, and the sense of walls, and the voicing they
provide, and my stillness here—unblinking—I am almost
                                        afraid
to move—and the litheness of this listening—
gossipy murmuring syllables now rushing up the scales,

but not really towards, not really away,
as if the thing deepened without increase,
the weight of the covers upon me,
the weight of the black, the slack and heaving argument
                                        of gravity—
and her quavering, lingering—
and him—what had been mossy
                suddenly clawed—
and everything now trying to arrive on time, ten thousand
                        invisible things all
braided in, fast—*appetite, the clatter of wheels upon tracks,
the rustling—what did I lose?—what was it
like?*—the weight of covers now upon me like the world's
                                        shut lid,
shut fast—not opening—
and cries, and cries, and something that will not come true.
When I stand up, pulling the heavy bedclothes back,
I want to open up the black.
Water sounds in the pipes between us.
A raised voice. Some steps.
More water in the singing pipes.
And scuffling. And the clicking of their light going off . . .
Debris of silences inside the silence.
Black gorged with absences. Room like an eyelid
                        spanked open
wide, I rip it, I rip it further—as if inside it now the million
tiny slippages could go to work, the whistling
                        of absence
where the thing *should care for us*—
where justice shifts and reshifts the bits to make
                        tomorrow—
tirelessly—kingdom of scribble and linger. . . . What do you

want, *you*, listening here with me now?   Inside the
                                    monologue,
what would you insert? What word?
What mark upon the pleating blacknesses of hotel air?
What, to open it? To make it hear you. To make it hear me.
How heavy can the singleness become?
Who will hear us? What shall we do?
I have waited all this time in the sooty minutes,
green gleaming bouquet offering and offering itself
right to my unrelenting open eyes,
long black arm tendering its icy blossoms up to me,
right through the blizzard of instances, the blurry
blacknesses, the whole room choked with the thousand spots
                            my glance has struck—
Long ago, long ago, and then, second-hand, this place
                            which is now,
whir—immortal? free?—glances like flames licking the walls . . .
Oh blackness, I am your servant. I take for mine your green, exactest,
                                    gift
in which you say yourself, in which you say
only yourself—

NOTES ON THE REALITY OF THE SELF

(Stanislavsky)

In time, when your sense of tempo will be more
firmly established, you will replace it
by a more delicate
mental beat.

(Even Grisha could not understand.)

This was repeated with syncopation.

Next we combined some beats, duples, triplets—
these heightened the tremulousness—
this in turn created new moods, corresponding emotions—
We varied the strength and kind of accent—

rich, thick, dry—then staccato or light—
the loud, the soft. These produced
the most contrasting moods. I lost track.
Syllables, words, speech, actions, movement in action—feelings,

right feelings—the clean dry beats of hands and feet—
love and jealousy—come into my room—the storm at sea—
once in the mountains—
headaches—
                gnawing mice—

us making mincemeat for the pie—

I lost my baggage. Where is the stationmaster.

Is there plenty of time?

The character being played
should not know what lies ahead—

He has no notion
of what the future has in store—

But how is it possible to forget what is coming?
How, when you play the part a thousand times?

(the pause has no concern for time) (it lasts)

Then my attention was drawn to a simple morning-coat.
It was made of some remarkable material I had never
                                        seen before—
a sand-colored, ruddy, grayish stuff,
covered with spots, dust, mixed in with ash.
An almost imperceptible sense of fatefulness stirred in me.
If one matched it with a hat, gloves—footgear,
all gray-red, speckled, faded, shadowy,
one would get the sinister, familiar effect.

The wardrobe attendants laid aside the coat for me.

Then there was nothing to do but leave,

the spotted morning-coat held in reserve for me.

But from that moment I existed but I was not I.
I listened but I did not hear.
I did not finish anything I undertook.
The question of who I was consumed me.

I became convinced I should not find the image
                        of the person that I
was: Seconds passed. What rose to the surface in me
plunged out of sight again. And yet I felt

the moment of my first investiture
was the moment I began to represent myself—
the moment I began to live—by degrees—second by
second—unrelentingly—Oh mind what you're doing!—

do you want to be *covered* or do you want to be *seen*?—

And the garment—how it becomes you!—starry
with the eyes of
others,
            weeping—

from Plato's PHAEDO

(AN ADAPTATION)

The truth rather is, that the soul which is pure at departing and draws after her no bodily taint, never having voluntarily during life had connection with the body, which she is ever avoiding, herself gathered into herself—and making such abstraction her perpetual study—which means, doesn't it, that she has been a true disciple of philosophy, and has in fact been always engaged in the practice of dying?—for is not philosophy the study of death?—

Certainly—

That soul, I say, herself invisible, departs to the invisible world—to the divine and immortal and rational; thither arriving, she is secure of bliss and is released from the error and folly of men, their fears and wild passions, and for ever dwells in company with the gods? Is this not true Cebes?

Yes, said Cebes, beyond a doubt.

But the soul which has been polluted, and is impure at the time of her departure, and is the companion and servant of the body always, and is in love with and fascinated by the body, until she is led to believe that the truth exists in a bodily form, which a man may touch and see and taste and use for his lusts—the soul, I mean, accustomed to hate and fear and avoid the intellectual principle, which to the bodily eye is dark and invisible—do you suppose that such a soul will depart pure and unalloyed?

Impossible, he replied.

She is held fast by the corporeal, which continual association and constant care of the body have wrought into her nature.

Very true.

And this corporeal element, my friend, is heavy and weighty and earthy and is the element of *sight* by which a soul is depressed and dragged down into the visible world because she is afraid of the invisible and of the world below—prowling about tombs and sepulchres, near which, as they tell us, are seen certain ghostly apparitions of souls which have not departed pure but are cloyed with sight—

That is very likely, Socrates.

Yes, that is very likely, Cebes . . .

From Brecht's
A SHORT ORGANUM FOR THE THEATRE

(AN ADAPTATION)

So that if we want to surrender ourselves to this great passion for reproducing, what ought our representations of men's life to look like? What is that attitude in face of nature and of society which we children of a scientific age would like to take up pleasurably in our theatre?

The attitude is a critical one. Faced with a river, it consists in regulating the river; faced with a fruit tree, in spraying the fruit tree; faced with movement, in constructing vehicles and aeroplanes; faced with society, in turning society upside-down . . .

For let us go into one of these theatre-houses and observe the effect which it has on the spectators, and we will see motionless figures in a peculiar condition. They stare at the stage as if in a trance: an expression which comes from the Middle Ages, the days of witches and priests. They seem relieved of activity, like men to whom something is being done. This detached state, where they seem to be given over to vague but profound sensations, grows deeper the better the work of the actors—and so we, as we do not approve of this situation, should like them to be as bad as possible—

You see, the theatre as we know it shows the *structure* of society (represented on the stage) as incapable of being influenced by society (in the auditorium). Oedipus, who offended, is executed: the gods see to that; they are beyond criticism. Shakespeare's great solitary figures, bearing on their breast the star of fate, carry through with irresistible force their futile and deadly outbursts; they prepare their own downfall; life, not death, becomes obscene as they collapse; the catastrophe is beyond criticism. Human sacrifices all round! Barbaric delights! We know that the barbarians have their art. Let us create another! Let

march ahead! Away with all obstacles! Since we seem to have landed in a battle, let us fight! Have we not seen how disbelief can move mountains?

It is not enough that we should have found that something is being kept from us? Before one thing and another there hangs a curtain: let us draw it up!

Our own period, which is transforming nature in so many ways, takes pleasure in understanding things so that we might interfere. There is a great deal to man, we say; so a great deal can be made out of him. He does not have to stay the way he is now, nor does he have to be seen only as he is now, but also as he might become. We must not start *with* him; we must start *on* him. This means that I must not simply set myself in his place, but must set myself facing him, to represent us all—which is why the theatre must alienate what it shows—

and why the actor must discard whatever means he has of getting the audience to identify itself with the characters which he plays. Aiming not to put his audience into a trance, he must not go into a trance himself. His muscles must remain loose. His way of speaking has to be free from all those cadences which lull the spectator. Even if he plays a man possessed he must not seem to be possessed himself—for how is the spectator to discover what possessed him if he does?—

and so at no moment must he go so far as to be wholly transformed into the character played—his feelings must not at bottom be those of the character, so that the audience's may not at bottom be those of the character either—(the audience must have complete freedom here)—

and there needs to be yet a further change in the actor's communication: just as the actor no longer has to persuade the audience that it is the author's character and not himself that is standing on the stage, so also he need not pretend that the events taking place on the stage have never been rehearsed, and are now happening for the first time . . . It should be apparent all through his performance that

even at the start and in the middle he knows how it ends—

(he must thus maintain a calm independence throughout)—

and even if empathy, or identification with the character, can be indulged in at rehearsals, it is something to be *absolutely* avoided in performance. For it is the crudest form of observation when the actor simply asks: what should I be *like*,

what should I be like if this or that were to happen to me? what?

ANNUNCIATION WITH A BULLET IN IT

(The dance has no name. It is a hungry dance.)

1

    There is a doorway in the air, a graduation
from nothing to nothing.
    A brief history of mankind.
A stammer between invisibles.
    The soft jingling of a chain.

    Wings pass through it. Something homeless.
As where an eyelid
    opening arrives instantly on
time at
    the world.
Blink.
    Are they continuous? *Two times two*

and then four walls, a window,
    proof, a lute—jingling—an
appetite . . . Forgive me,

    there is a doorway through which we must pass
together,
    you and I.
Made of words it sounds like "what-if-nothing." Of flesh,
    an eyeblink, mossy. Of the
world, something off
    the flying bird gone on—the arc—something infinitesimal

though seething with little facts—
    a doorway of little facts seething—

66

2

You must find it.
        You must be merciless and find it.
The secret in it. Graffiti on air. Wingscrape. Listen—
        a single note is hurled
onto the evening air.
        A man's name? A low quick shriek?
A screen-door slams beneath.
        House-shake.
Stillness.
        Ravens cawing overhead . . .

And on the rug tonight, holding our dog someone has shot,
        large, black and white, long-haired, near death,
whispering the few commands it knows as praise—*stay, stay*—
        I happen to glance up out the window placed
just above the two of us
        at something seen through the empty tree out there—

my hand stroking his unconscious head,
        jingling his name-and-registration
by mistake—

3

Like a crust on something, that sky—
        something down here somewhat viscous, blinking—
a crust forming to seal us off—
        hiss of the heating system switching on—
moonlight on fur and fingers in it, caressing—

4

     FEAR NOT says the angel
of air,
     a bullioned slant on the emptiness
I reach my hand into.
     FEAR NOT or so I think where my fingers

feel themselves *lessen* and the invisible *thicken* . . .

The weight was coming from out-side.
     A sleekness removed from the shifting rest of things.
Something glass-like I can make out—a palm? an eye?—
     some pressure in the dust?—
FEAR NOT (loud in the air)—
     and more disturbance on the dust—lipmarks? fingermarks?—
(but not *letters*) (I tried to read),
     out through the window now smoke from the neighbor's stack
                           moving off
aslant
     (me watching it closely) (for *a time*) but then

FEAR NOT and I look
     back—day *breaking* now, corners pushed free, outlines
cut clean,
     confusion coalescing and settling, dust-like, into this
apparition: the room (I notice myself
     nodding to the room):
chair, four-poster bed, 16-pane window in
     its frame—
     a violent stillness—
as if it had all suddenly just *taken place*—
     it the angel, *it* the seizing up of the great reverber-
                           ation into this

place FEAR NOT—my left hand feeling the spun-wool blanket round
                                          the dog—
        right down in the nailtip—
warp, filament—
        every now and then a knot—
and how *I* must be the passage
        through,

up through the hand,
        and the light in through my eyes,
and the scent of the lilacs in the glass vase from Venice,
        and the color in too (4 distinct purples),
and the faceted convexity of the reddish glass,

        and *Venice* too (20 years ago),
                              that man's long voice

        still screaming at us from the passing boat—

        then the louder plash of our single oar—drowning him out—

        all of it searing really—

        so that I have to sit very very still,
light brightening,
        in it the soft jingling of a chain,
a chatter of wheels upon tracks . . .

                              5

Then she said "it is Sunday May 28 my birthday.
        I am celebrating packing for the long journey.
A youthful SS man, blond, like an angel, just informed us

                              69

we are to rise at 4 a.m. for the journey.
Anyone not up at four a.m. will get a *Kugel*.
    A bullet simply for not getting up?

                                6

    Mother's face, her eyes, cannot be described.
She knows there is nothing beyond this.
    She keeps smiling at me I can't stand it.
I am silently pleading with her: *stop smiling*.
    I gaze at her tenderly and smile back.

                                7

Six months, four of us are still alive,
    there is a sudden selection.
Rachel, our little sister, will not possibly be able to make it.
    She is all too ready.
It cannot happen.
    Mengele is selecting a little distance away.
Frantically, we try to make Rachel healthier looking,

older looking.
    One of us has a piece of cloth.
We place it on Rachel's head as a kerchief.
    We make her stand on her tiptoes—(she pleads she has no
strength for such superhuman
    efforts)—we pinch her face
to an unnatural
    redness. We pinch her and pinch her.
Mengele passes her by.
    This day the oven has been cheated of our precious sister.

8

We touch each other,
    Cipi, Chicha, Rachel, Isabella. We seem to be alive.
Words come out of our lips, we must be alive.
    The Germans look like things we have seen before.
We are not sure they are real.

9

We are marching in the blizzard.
    To be five in the row is the prisoners' responsibility.
So we have to find an unattached girl.
    Always when we find one it is never permanent.
Sooner or later she is taken to the crematorium.
    It is a constant struggle—

10

    Rachel is coughing up badly—
On one foot she has a torn leather shoe on the other a Dutch
                                    wooden one—
    in the blizzard she can barely drag herself along—
between the four of us we are missing one shoe—
    whichever one tries to aid Rachel by giving up a shoe
will be the one to be taken—
    in the past we have always found
some kind of solution—

11

    The little baby born yesterday
is now off to the ovens—

We all touch the little one before she is wrapped in
the piece of paper
        and handed over to
the Blockelteste—

                        12

. . . lord, the *Oberscharführer* will choose me, I know he will.
        I can dig the grave, but please, please don't choose me to
                                carry the body.
I am just a child.
        I cannot carry the dead body.
Have mercy.
        The cold dead body I cannot touch."

                        13

Said the angel,
        I have analyzed thousands of documents,
I have tirelessly pursued specialists and historians, tirelessly,
        I have tried in vain to find a single former deportee

capable of proving to me that he had really seen
        with his own eyes
a gas chamber
                TIRELESSLY
(wingprint in dust) (smoke) the

only acceptable proof that it was used to kill
        is that one died from it—
(tirelessly)—
        but if one is dead one cannot testify

                        72

that it is
　　on account of such a chamber—

　　there is, therefore, no gas chamber
(Fear not)
　　there is, therefore, no place that can be identified
as a gas chamber
　　　　　　(Fear not)
　　therefore one has been fooled as to the existence
of gas chambers
　　　　　　(Fear not)

Then (lifting) (dust-swirl in the room)

　　a plaintiff is someone who has incurred damages
and who disposes of the means to prove it,

　　one becomes a victim
if one loses those means

　　　　　FEAR NOT

14

Once in this room—
　　I was a child of ten. It was winter, afternoon.
There was a dark green velvet couch where now there are
　　　　　　　　　　this rug, this dog.
　　Someone was humming a half-remembered tune
—the window let it in—
　　sometimes she hummed—sometimes the words surfaced
and a phrase . . .
　　Hear her soul go up

73

into the words—
    the lover by the stream,
the girl in summer—then
    subside, the song back down
into the hands,
    clothesclips snapping

onto the long free line . . .
    I settled deeper into the pillowy green.
The hum disappeared, or so it seemed.
    I was holding a paperback copy of *Anna Karenin*,
the print very small—

    I looked at the girl on the cover again.
Swift whirr of heating ducts clicking off.
    Trucks going by beyond the wall.
Clink of utensils being stacked.
    One phrase sung out—soft
jingling—events . . .

    When Anna walks into the well-lit room,
black velvet dress, whiteness of shoulders bared, Vronski's eyes
    fall suddenly on her so that her *being*
seen is
    born. I tried to see past her. But her black waist

    blocked the whole view,

    black hourglass the stillness would use to enter,
swirling, breathless,
    yet in itself nothing,
not fear, not desire (I knew that even then),

not hope, not even an awakening—just

a rip where evidence exists,

   but not *of* anything,

a wing of singed bits,
      made of the glances that reach it,
swirling yet very still,
      a name in the continuous hum,
a scratch in the dust where only light seems to have pressed,
      ticking, twirling, incredibly still, I squint, I cannot see

the words, it's all
      one universal, stubborn black
out of which—*in* which?—the dark words *seem*,
      overlapping layers of them—rows—as feathers on a wing
                  are packed—I rub

my eyes, humming gone too, green gone
      where velvet was,
although I feel my
      weight on it—nothing coming from *outside*—
the whole room swirling—
      distant music or is it
a chain—even the window gone

   though blacks still swarm there, many-eyed—

and many-eyed and many-limbed the black where the page

   had been—(I think,

perhaps I am the word inside the glance that picks me up?)—
while in a corner now the black begins (*I will be read?*) to rip,
letting what lustrous thing leak in? an eye? a name?—
why are you reading in the dark?—
it's night, darling; it's dinnertime—

15

The second night the dog woke up.
Raised his head as if in a sudden hurry.
We tried to keep him still but he wanted to walk.
Tried very slowly, roaming, wanting to go elsewhere.
We thought it miraculous, that it meant something.
That he should live with the bullet in his heart.
We watched him very carefully.
Clinking of tags from room to room.

Icy the star I watched above him as he took a few steps
in the yard.
Meaning? meaning? shrieked the small facts, the clinking
gleaming chain of them,

the parts of wings whirring like a heating system—close in,
far off—

the hum of my listening—

the whirring like an appetite—an engine's appetite—fear not—

16

And the third night? And the fourth? And then? And then?

17

"Oh but here is a piece of bread said Chicha—
     Please eat it—Please please make
yourself live—

You must not think I took it from myself—

I really really am not hungry—"

from Sir Francis Bacon's NOVUM ORGANUM

(AN ADAPTATION)

We took a metal bell, of a light and thin sort, such as is used for saltcellars, and immersed it in a basin of water, so as to carry the air contained in its interior down with it to the bottom of the basin. We had first, however, placed a small globe at the bottom of the basin, over which we placed the bell. The result was, that if the globe were small compared with the interior of the bell, the air would contract itself, and be compressed without being forced out, but if it were too large for the air readily to yield to it, the latter became impatient of the pressure, raised the bell partly up, and ascended in bubbles.

We took a glass egg, with a small hole at one end; we drew out the air by violent suction at this hole, and then closed the hole with the finger, immersed the egg in water, and then removed the finger. The air being constrained by the effort made in suction, and dilated beyond its natural state, and therefore striving to recover and contract itself (so that if the egg had not been immersed in water, it would have drawn in the air with a hissing sound), now drew in a sufficient quantity of water to allow the air to recover its former dimensions.

We took a leaden globe . . .

ON DESIRE

(*from Benjamin Whorf's* LANGUAGE, THOUGHT, AND REALITY)

(AN ADAPTATION)

The Hopi metaphysics imposes upon the universe two grand cosmic forms, which as a first approximation in terminology we may call MANIFESTED and MANIFESTING (or, UNMANIFEST) or, again, OBJECTIVE and SUBJECTIVE. The objective or manifested comprises all that is or has been accessible to the senses, the historical physical universe, with no attempt to distinguish between present and past, but excluding everything that we call future. The subjective or manifesting comprises all that we call future, BUT NOT MERELY THIS; it includes equally and indistinguishably all that we call mental—everything that appears or exists in the mind—the striving of purposeful desire toward manifestation. It is the realm of expectancy and purpose, of efficient causes, of thought thinking itself out from an inner realm into manifestation. It is in a dynamic state, yet not a state of motion—it is not advancing towards us out of a future, but ALREADY WITH US; its dynamism evolving without motion from the subjective by degrees to a result which is the objective. . . .

If we were to approximate our metaphysical terminology more closely to Hopian terms, we should probably speak of the subjective realm as the realm of HOPE or HOPING. Every language contains terms that crystallize in themselves the basic postulates of an unformulated philosophy in which is couched the thought of a people. Such are our words "reality, substance, matter, cause." Such a term in Hopi is the word most often translated "hope"—*tunátya*—"it is in the action of hoping, it hopes, it is hoped for, it thinks or is thought of with hope," etc. Most metaphysical words in Hopi are verbs, not nouns as in European languages. The verb *tunátya* contains in its idea of hope something of our words "thought," "desire," and "cause," which sometimes must be used to translate it.

THE DREAM OF THE UNIFIED FIELD

1

On my way to bringing you the leotard
you forgot to include in your overnight bag,
the snow started coming down harder.
I watched each gathering of leafy flakes
melt round my footfall.
I looked up into it—late afternoon but bright.
Nothing true or false in itself. Just motion. Many strips of
motion. Filaments of falling marked by the tiny certainties
of flakes. Never blurring yet themselves a cloud. Me in it
                              and yet
moving easily through it, black Lycra leotard balled into
                              my pocket,
your tiny dream in it, my left hand on it or in it
                    to keep
warm. Praise this. Praise that. Flash a glance up and try
                         to see
the arabesques and runnels, gathering and loosening, as they
define, as a voice would, the passaging through from
                         the-other-than-
human. Gone as they hit the earth. But embellishing.
Flourishing. The road with me on it going on through. In-
scribed with the present. As if it really
were possible to exist, and exist, never to be pulled back
in, given and given never to be received. The music
of the footfalls doesn't stop, doesn't
mean. *Here are your things*, I said.

2

Starting home I heard—bothering, lifting, then
                    bothering again—

the huge flock of starlings massed over our
                              neighborhood
these days; heard them lift and
swim overhead through the falling snow
as though the austerity of a true, cold thing, a verity,
the black bits of their thousands of bodies swarming
                              then settling
overhead. I stopped. All up and down the empty oak
they stilled. Every limb sprouting. Every leafy backlit
                              body
filling its part of the empty crown. I tried to count—
then tried to estimate—
but the leaves of this wet black tree at the heart of
                              the storm—shiny—
river through limbs, back onto the limbs,
scatter, blow away, scatter, recollect—
undoing again and again the tree without it ever ceasing to be
                              full.
Foliage of the tree of the world's waiting.
Of having waited a long time and
                  still having
to wait. Of trailing and screaming.
Of engulfed readjustments. Of blackness redisappearing
                              into
downdrafts of snow. Of indifference. Of indifferent
                              reappearings.
                  I think of you
back of me now in the bright house of
                  your friend
twirling in the living room in the shiny leotard
                              you love.
I had looked—as I was leaving—through the window

to see you, slick in your magic,
pulling away from the wall—

I watch the head explode then recollect, explode, recollect.

3

Then I heard it, inside the swarm, the single cry

of the crow. One syllable—one—inside the screeching and the
                                                    skittering,
inside the constant repatterning of a thing not nervous yet
                                          not ever
still—but not uncertain—without obedience
yet not without law—one syllable—
black, shiny, twirling on its single stem,
rooting, one foot on the earth,
twisting and twisting—

and then again—a little further off this time—*down the
ravine*, a voice inside a head, filling a head. . . .

See, my pocket is empty now. I let my hand
open and shut in there. I do it again. Two now, skull and
                                          pocket
with their terrified inhabitants.

   You turn the music up. The window nothing to you, liquid, dark,
where now your mother has come back to watch.

4

Closeup, he's blue—streaked iris blue, india-ink blue—and
black—an oily, firey set of blacks—none of them
true—as where hate and order touch—something that cannot
become known. Stages of black but without
graduation. So there is no direction.
All of this happened, yes. Then disappeared
into the body of the crow, chorus of meanings,
layers of blacks, then just the crow, plain, big,
lifting his claws to walk thrustingly
forward and back—indigo, cyanine, beryl, grape, steel . . . Then suddenly he
wings and—braking as he lifts
the chest in which an eye-sized heart now beats—
—he's up—a blunt clean stroke—
one ink-streak on the early evening snowlit scene—
See the gesture of the painter?—Recall the
crow?—Place him quickly on his limb as he comes sheering in,
close to the trunk, to land—Is he now
disappeared again?

5

. . . .*long neck, up, up with the head,*
eyes on the fingertips, bent leg, shift of
the weight—*turn*—No, no, begin again . . .
What had she seen, Madame Sakaroff, at Stalingrad, now in
her room of mirrors tapping her cane
as the piano player begins the interrupted Minuet again
and we line up right foot extended, right
                              hand extended, the Bach mid-phrase—
Europe? The dream of Europe?—midwinter afternoon,

rain at the windowpane, ceilings at thirty feet and coffered
floating over the wide interior spaces . . .
No one must believe in God again I heard her say
one time when I had come to class too soon
and had been sent to change. The visitor had left,
kissing her hand, small bow, and I had seen her (from the curtain)
(having forgotten I was there)
turn from the huge pearl-inlaid doors she had just closed,
one hand still on the massive, gold, bird-headed knob,
and see—a hundred feet away—herself—a woman in black in
                              a mirrored room—
saw her not shift her gaze but bring her pallid tensile hand—
as if it were not part of her—slowly down from
the ridged, cold, feathered knob and, recollected, fixed upon
                              that other woman, emigrée,
begin to move in stiffly towards her . . . You out there
                                        now,
you in here with me—I watched the two of them,
black and black, in the gigantic light,
glide at each other, heads raised, necks long—
me wanting to cry out—where were the others?—wasn't it late?
the two of her like huge black hands—
clap once and once only and the signal is given—
but to what?—regarding what?—till closer-in I saw
                              more suddenly
how her eyes eyed themselves: no wavering:
like a vast silver page burning: the black hole
                    expanding:
like a meaning coming up quick from inside that page—
coming up quick to seize the reading face—
each face wanting the other to *take* it—
but where? and *from* where?—I was eight—

I saw the different weights of things,
saw the vivid performance of the present,
saw the light rippling almost shuddering where her body finally
                                            touched
the image, the silver film between them like something that would have
                                            shed itself in nature now
but wouldn't, couldn't, here, on tight,
between, not thinning, not slipping off to let some
                                            seed-down
through, no signal in it, no information . . . Child,
                        what should I know
to save you that I do not know, hands on this windowpane?—

6

The storm: I close my eyes and,
standing in it, try to make it *mine*. An inside
thing. Once I was. . . . once, once.
It settles, in my head, the wavering white
sleep, the instances—they stick, accrue,
grip up, connect, they do not melt,
I will not let them melt, they build, cloud and cloud,
I feel myself weak, I feel the thinking muscle-up—
outside, the talk-talk of the birds—outside,
strings and their roots, leaves inside the limbs,
in some spots the skin breaking—
but inside, no more exploding, no more smoldering, no more,
inside, a splinter colony, new world, possession
gripping down to form,
wilderness brought deep into my clearing,
out of the ooze of night,
limbed, shouldered, necked, visaged, the white—

now the clouds coming in (don't look up),
now the Age behind the clouds, The Great Heights,
all in there, reclining, eyes closed, huge,
centuries and centuries long and wide,
and underneath, barely attached but attached,
like a runner, my body, my tiny piece of
the century—minutes, houses going by—The Great
                                    Heights—
anchored by these footsteps, now and now,
the footstepping—now and now—carrying its vast
white sleeping geography—mapped—
not a lease—*possession*—"At the hour of vespers
in a sudden blinding snow,
they entered the harbor and he named it Puerto de

7

San Nicolas and at its entrance he imagined he
                                    could see
its beauty and goodness, *sand right up to the land*
where you can put the side of a ship. He thought
                                    he saw
Indians fleeing through the white before
the ship . . . As for him, he did not believe what his
                                    crew
told him, nor did he understand them well, nor they
him. In the white swirl, he placed a large cross
                        at the western side of
the harbor, on a conspicuous height,
as a sign that Your Highness claim the land as
Your own. After the cross was set up,
three sailors went into the bush (immediately erased

from sight by the fast snow) to see what kinds of
trees. They captured three very black Indian
women—one who was young and pretty.
The Admiral ordered her clothed and returned her to
                                        her land

courteously. There her people told
that she had not wanted to leave the ship,
but wished to stay on it. The snow was wild.
Inside it, though, you could see
this woman was wearing a little piece of
gold on her nose, which was a sign there was
                                        gold

on that land"—

from Audubon's MISSOURI RIVER JOURNALS

(AN ADAPTATION)

June 4, Sunday. We have run pretty well, though the wind has been tolerably high; the country we have passed this day is somewhat better than what we saw yesterday . . .

We passed this morning the old Riccaree Village, where General Ashley was so completely beaten as to lose eighteen of his men, with the very weapons and ammunition that he had trafficked with the Indians of that village, against all the remonstrances of his friends and interpreters; yet he said that it proved fortunate for him, as he turned his steps towards some other spot, where he procured one hundred packs of Beaver skins for a mere song.

We are now fast for the night at an abandoned post, or fort, of the Company, where, luckily for us, a good deal of wood was found cut. We saw only one Wolf, and a few small gangs of Buffaloes. Bell shot a Bunting which resembles Henslow's, but we have no means of comparing it at present. By the way, I forgot to say that along with the three Prairie Marmots, he shot also four Spoon-billed Ducks, which we ate at dinner to-day, and found delicious. Bell saw many Lazuli Finches this morning and notwithstanding the tremendous shaking of our boat, Sprague managed to draw four figures of the legs and feet of the Wolf shot by Bell yesterday, and my own pencil was not idle.

June 5, Monday. In the course of the morning we passed Cannon Ball River, and the very remarkable bluffs about it, of which we cannot well speak until we have stopped there and examined their nature. We saw two Swans alighting on the prairie at a considerable distance. We stopped to take wood at Bowie's settlement, at which place his wife was killed by some of the Riccaree Indians. The Indians took parts of her hair and went off. She was duly buried; but the Gros Ventres returned some time afterwards, took up the body, and carried off the balance of her hair. We have also passed Apple Creek. At one place where the bluffs were high, we saw five Buffaloes landing a few hundred yards above us on the western side; one of them cantered off immediately, and by some means did reach the top of the hills, and went out of our sight; the four others ran, waded, and swam at different places, always above us, trying to make their escape. At one spot they attempted to climb the bluff, having unconsciously passed the place where their leader had made good his way, and in their attempts to scramble up, tumbled down, and at last became so much affrighted that they took to the river for good, with the intention to swim to the shore they had left. The moment they began to swim we were all about the boat with guns and rifles, awaiting the instant when they would be close under our bows. The moment came; I was on the lower deck among several of the people with guns, and the firing was soon heavy; but not one of the Buffaloes was stopped, although every one must have been severely hit and wounded. Bell shot a load of buckshot at the head of one, which disappeared entirely under the water for perhaps a minute. I sent a ball through the neck of the last of the four, but all ineffectually, and off they went, swimming to the opposite shore; one lagged behind the rest, but, having found footing on a sand-bar, it rested awhile, and again swam off to rejoin its companions. They all reached the shore, but were quite as badly off on that side as they had been on the other, and their difficulties must have been great indeed; however, in a short time we had passed them. Mr. Charles Primeau, who is a good shot, and who killed the young Buffalo bull the other day, assured me that it was his opinion the whole of these would die before sundown. Also have seen Geese, and Goslings, Ravens, Blue Herons, Bluebirds, Thrushes, Redheaded Woodpeckers and Red-shafted Ditto, Martins, an immense number of Rough-winged Swallows about their holes, and Barn Swallows. We heard Killdeers last evening. Small Crested Flycatchers, Summer Yellow-birds, Maryland Yellow-throats, and House Wrens are seen as we pass along our route; while the Spotted Sandpiper accompanies us all along the river. Sparrow Hawks, Turkey Buzzards, Arctic Towhee Buntings, Cat-birds, Mallards, Coots, Gadwalls, King-birds, Yellow-breasted Chats, Red Thrushes, all are noted as we pass. The wind has been cold, and this evening we have had a dash of rain.

June 7, Wednesday. We saw more Indians than at any previous time since leaving St. Louis; and it is possible that there are a hundred huts, made of mud, all looking like so many potato winter-houses in the Eastern States. As soon as we were near the shore, every article that could conveniently be carried off was placed under lock and key, and our division door was made fast, as well as those of our own rooms. Even the axes and poles were put by. Our captain told us that last year they stole his cap and his shot-pouch and horn, and that it was through the interference of the first chief that he recovered his cap and horn; but that a squaw had his leather belt, and would not give it up. The appearance of these poor, miserable devils, as we approached the shore, was wretched enough. There they stood in the pelting rain and keen wind, covered with Buffalo robes, red blankets, and the like, some partially and most curiously besmeared with mud; and as they came on board, and we shook hands with each of them, I felt a clamminess that rendered the ceremony most repulsive. Their legs and naked feet were covered with mud. They looked at me with apparent curiosity, perhaps on account of my beard, which produced the same effect at Fort Pierre. They all looked very poor; and our captain says they are the *ne plus ultra* of thieves. It is said there are nearly three thousand men, women, and children that, during winter, cram themselves into these miserable hovels. Harris and I walked to the fort about nine o'clock. The walking was rascally, passing through mud and water the whole way. The yard of the fort itself was as bad. We entered Mr. Chardon's own room, crawled up a crazy ladder, and in a low garret I had the great pleasure of seeing alive the Swift or Kit Fox which he has given to me. It ran swiftly from one corner to another, and, when approached, growled somewhat in the manner of a common Fox. Mr. Chardon told me that good care would be taken of it until our return, that it would be chained to render it more gentle . . .

June 8, Thursday. This morning was fair and cold, as you see by the range of the thermometer, 37 degrees to 56 degrees. We started at a very early hour, and breakfasted before five, on account of the village of Gros Ventres, where our captain had to stop. We passed a few lodges belonging to the tribe of the Mandans, about all that remained. I only counted eight, but am told there are twelve. We saw a crippled and evidently tame Wolf, and two Indians, following us on the top of the hills. We saw two Swans on a bar, and a female Elk, with her young fawn, for a few minutes. I wished that we had been ashore, as I know full well that the mother would not leave her young; and the mother killed, the young one would have been easily caught alive. We are now stopping for the night, and our men are cutting wood. We have done this, I believe, four times to-day, and have run upwards of sixty miles. At the last wood-cutting place, a young leveret was started by the men, and after a short race, the thing squatted, and was killed by the stroke of a stick. It proved to be the young of *Lepus townsendii* [*L. campestris*], large enough to have left the mother, and weighing rather more than a pound. It is a very beautiful specimen. The eyes are very large, and the iris pure amber color. Its hair is tightly, but beautifully curled. Its measurements are as follows. . . .

June 9, Friday. Thermometer 42 degrees, 75 degrees, 66 degrees. We had a heavy white frost last night, but we have had a fine, pleasant day on the whole. We passed the Little Missouri (the real one) about ten this morning. It is a handsome stream, that runs all the way from the Black Hills, one of the main spurs of the mighty Rocky Mountains. We saw three Elks swimming across it, and the number of this fine species of Deer that are about us now is almost inconceivable. We have heard of burning springs, which we intend to examine on our way down. We started a Goose from the shore that had evidently young ones; she swam off, beating the water with wings half extended, until nearly one hundred yards off. A shot from a rifle was fired at her, and missed. Afterwards the trappers shot at two Geese with two young ones. We landed at four o'clock, and Harris and Bell shot some Bay-winged Buntings and *Emberiza pallida*, whilst Sprague and I went up to the top of the hills, bounding the beautiful prairie, by which we had stopped to repair something about the engine. We gathered some handsome lupines, of two different species, and many other curious plants. From this elevated spot we could see the wilderness to an immense distance; the Missouri looked as if only a brook, and our steamer a very small one indeed. At this juncture we saw two men running along the shore upwards, and I supposed they had seen an Elk or something else, of which they were in pursuit. Meantime, gazing around, we saw a large lake, where we are told that Ducks, Geese, and Swans breed in great numbers; this we intend also to visit when we come down. At this moment I heard the report of a gun from the point where the men had been seen, and when we reached the steamboat, we were told that a Buffalo had been killed. From the deck I saw a man swimming round the animal; he got on its side, and floated down the stream with it. The captain sent a parcel of men with a rope; the swimmer fastened this round the neck of the Buffalo, and with his assistance, for he now swam all the way, the beast was brought alongside; and as the tackle had been previously fixed, it was hauled up on the fore deck. Sprague took its measurements with me, which are as follows: length from nose to root of tail, 8 feet; height of fore shoulder to hoof, 4 ft. 9½ in.; height at the rump to hoof, 4 ft. 2 in. The head was cut off, as well as one fore and one hind foot. The head is so full of symmetry, and so beautiful, that I shall have a drawing of it to-morrow, as well as careful ones of the feet.

Whilst cutting wood was going on, we went ashore. Bell shot at two Buffaloes out of eight, and killed both; he would also have shot a Wolf, had he had more bullets. Harris saw, and shot at, an Elk; but he knows little about still hunting, and thereby lost a good chance. A negro fire-tender went off with his rifle and shot two of Townsend's Hares. One was cut in two by his ball, and he left it on the ground; the other was shot near the rump, and I have it now hanging before me; and, let me tell you, that I never before saw so beautiful an animal of the same family. My drawing will be a good one; it is a fine specimen, an old male.

2.151   Pictorial form is the possibility that things are related to one another in the same way as the elements of the picture.

2.1511   *That* is how a picture is attached to reality; it reaches right out to it.

2.1512   It is laid against reality like a measure.

2.15121   Only the end-points of the graduating lines actually *touch* the object that is to be measured.

2.1513   So a picture, conceived in this way, also includes the pictorial relationship, which makes it into a picture.

2.1514   The pictorial relationship consists of the correlations of the picture's elements with things.

2.1515   These correlations are, as it were, the feelers of the picture's elements, with which the picture touches reality.

2.16   If a fact is to be a picture, it must have something in common with what it depicts.

2.161   There must be something identical in a picture and what it depicts, to enable the one to be a picture of the other at all.

2.17   What a picture must have in common with reality, in order to be able to depict it—correctly or incorrectly—in the way it does, is its pictorial form.

2.171   A picture can depict any reality whose form it has.
A spatial picture can depict anything spatial, a coloured one
anything coloured, etc.

2.172   A picture cannot, however, depict its pictorial form: it dis-
plays it.

MANIFEST DESTINY

"In the center of Georgiana's left cheek there was a singular mark, deeply interwoven, as it were, with the texture and substance of her face. . . ."
(HAWTHORNE)

1

(Pink Palace Museum, Memphis)

She lifts the bullet out of the blazing case.
Here.
  What can it harm?
Clock on the wall.
  Ceiling-fan on.
Earlier it was

muzzleflash, dust. All round in the woods
  voices and orders but you can't be sure whose.
Here's a sunken place by the road for
  shelter, for the speechless
reload.

  Tents that way or is it fog?
Or is it freedom?
  A horse with his dead man
disappears.
  The line is *where* that has to be maintained at all

cost?
  Smoke clears and here's
a thousand peachtrees,
  a massacre of blooms, or is it smoke?
The fire is let go, travels into the blossoming (not as fast
  as you'd

95

think) enters a temple then a thigh.
    Carrying one body into the other.
She holds up the set of knives in their calfskin case.
    Behind her the diorama where the field surgeon's
sawing.
    There's the wax mouth held shut.
There's the scream inside—gold, round.
    Peachblossoms fall.
No chloroform so whiskey's

    used and sometimes—now lifting up out of the
incandescent case—the
    bullet we bend close
to see the
    bitemarks on—three dark impressions—whose footprints
on bottomland—
    whose 8,000 bodies, sticky with blossom, loosening into the wet
                                   field,
the still-living moving the more

    obedient bodies of the already-dead
up and down during the night,
    petals continuing to cover them.
Flashes of lightning showed hogs feeding on the dead says the
    captain who hears the wounded rebel under him say "oh
God what made You

    come down here to fight? we never
would have come up there."
    Look, he lives to write it down.
Here are the black words photographed and blown
    up wall-size behind
the guide.

Do you think these words are still enough?
And the next thing and the next thing?
    Where is the mark that stays?
Where is what makes a mark

that stays?
    What's *real* slides through.
The body rots. The body won't hold it.
    Here's the next room and the *flight simulator*.
We the living run our arms along the grooves as we walk through.
    They are lifted and dropped.
Experience wingaction.
    I shut my eyes and try it

again.
    The museum hums round me.
Something else,
    something niggardly letting the walls stay up for now, hums,
something speechless and dense and stationary letting

    matter coalesce
in obstinate illustration—hums.
    Hear the theories come to cloak it—buzz.
Hear the deafness all over the trees, green.
    Hear his scream go into the light.
See how the light is untouched
    by the scream that
enters it.
    Dust motes.
Peachblossom-fall.

    Where shall the scream stick?
What shall it dent?

Won't the deafness be cracked?
Won't the molecules be loosened?

Are you listening? We need the scream to leave its mark
on the silky down of
the petalled
light—

2
(Peach Orchard, Shiloh Battlefield)
(Mississippi River)

She's the scream he's the light.
They are playing, sort of, at Leda and Swan.

No, she's the *stream* he's the *blossomfall*?

Do you think these words are still enough?

Something out there on a spot in the middle of the
river.

Where the sun hits first and most directly.

Where there's a little gash on the waterfilm.

An indentation almost a cut his foothold.

Her a stream, yes, though not less a girl,
him the light become winged in its lower reaches,
almost biting the water there where it touches

or so the story goes—

him needing something he did not have,

(all round them the confused clickings of matter)—

the insects whining high, whining low . . .

He wants to go into her, he goes through.

Can't seem to find her: can't seem to find her.

The more he enters the more she disappears.

Can't seem to find her, can't seem to find her.

The insects whining high, and whining low.

The toothed light down hard on the sinewy scream.

She is asking for it he is not there.

He is promising forever she is not there.

Do I own you she says—

Yes, yes he is not there—

She is rising up as he descends then she
        is not
there then she
        is water beneath him, a river is flowing

he's clawing for foothold the river won't take his mark—

Where she eddies it's brighter for an instant—
Where the scream is, the light is broken for
                    the instant—
Where the light is brighter the scream is
                    the instant—
Where they thought they could marry—
In which they thought they could touch
                    each other—
The instant: they can't see it: a scent: in it
    the place something maybe took

place but what—

How can the scream rise up out of its grave of matter?
How can the light drop down out of its grave of thought?

How can they cross over and the difference between them swell with
existence?

Everything at the edges of everything else now rubbing,

making tiny sounds that add up to laughter,

something the breeze can lift and drop,

something that clots here and there and confirms our
fear,

(and the laughter which you might *think* is an angel
above them)

(a body whose ribs are the limits of everything)

(oh but we are *growing* now that there's a hurry, aren't we?)

(here where nothing is alive and vastly limbed and eyed)

(and the future spreads before us the back of its long
                                        body)

For the first time since Homer . . . whispers his open book,
spine up to the light

and *Naturalism was already outmoded when* . . .

and *by visible truth we mean the apprehension of* . . .

3

Beautiful natural blossoms . . .

    What is this she lifts and puts into my palm,
this leaden permanence—ash
    of a man's scream still
intact?
    Strange how heavy it is I think.
And here are the in-

    dentations—
I run my finger in them,
    little consequence, firmer than the cause.

    The war is gone. The reason gone. The body gone. Its
reason gone. The name the face the personal
    identity and yet here

is a pain that will not
    diminish . . .
I stand with my hand out in front of me.
    Someone lifts the thing slightly

then puts it back down.
    I'm looking for contagion. I'm watching the face

    of my friend as he tries to see
deeply the bitten bullet without
    lifting his hand to touch.
I watch his eyes focus.
    I watch him try to see what there is to
see.
    The russet cord behind him gleams.
The ceiling fan.
    The woman's voice.
The windows to the
    left and through it

    blossoms in rain.
Little mist,
    you take the sunlight and its frequency,
which is a color, in,
    you have these teeth which are molecules,
and in them there is
    a form of desire

which ascertains what color of the light
    will do, into which then the molecules must bite
down, taking the necessary
    nutrient—color? speed?—

into themselves and,
    altering, matter

make—white and silky by virtue of what they
    do not
apprehend—

What does this young man's bite into the world
    take—
what nutrient
    does his bite find,

    what grows, white and airy and almost invisible,
out of him
    as of this
feeding?
    Here is the young man's great-grandfather himself a young man
getting off the boat
    in James Town, 1754, with a sack of seeds.

This is a peach seed. It has come from Amsterdam.
    Before it was in a crate unloaded in Venice.
A new thing for the human mind—a peach.
    Found in Baghdad by another young man.
Tasted out of curiosity.
    Here the spring of 1762 and the first blossoms,

    then a good summer, not much war, then the first
fruit.
    Here the wife's face, he is handing her a fruit.
She puts the churn down a minute. The child is crying.
    Here, he says, try it. And her mouth

over the rough skin, the fire
    needing attention, the child
starting to scream.
    Here the mark on the surface of that

peach.
    Here the note she puts in her journal
that night.
    The words for it—that taste.
The season it stands at the heart of, that
    sweetness not entirely sweet.
A fruit part sunshine part water she writes.
    But what she's thinking is his face when he came into the room

holding it
    this morning. What was it
he held in his hand
    that his face
could not see
    could not hold?

Is he sick, or is he well
Is he young, or is he old
Is he rich, or is he poor
Did you say valor, or value
Did you say statute, or statue
Did he act properly?   Improperly?
Did he?   Did he?

Did *you* walk into the city yesterday?
Did you *walk* into the city yesterday?
Did you walk into the *city* yesterday?
Did you walk into the city *yesterday*?

Man wants but little here below
Man wants but little here below

Do not say *chile* for child; *feller* for fellow;
fuss for first; *kinely* for kindly

Do not say *loss* for lost; *burs* for burst;
juss for just; *greates* for greatest

Did you go into the city yesterday?

Did he behave properly or improperly?
Are there living or dead?
Is he rich or poor?

Did you go into the city yesterday?

Do not say *monuch* for monarch; *fo-res*
for forest; *a-cun* for acorn

(From what does an oak tree grow? How is it
nourished?)
(Where is the rising inflection marked? What is
the rule?)

They *reefed* the topsails.
He *quenched* a flame.
She *laughs* at him.
A *frame* of adamant.

Thy *lookest from thy throne* in the clouds

and *laugh'st* at the storm. All clothed

in rags the infant lay. Do not

say *smokin* for smoking, *clearin* for clearing,

ketchin for catching, *spinnin* for spinning

The busy wife by the open door
was turning at the spinning wheel
(do not say *mine* for mind) (do not say *an*

for *and*) (and *shame* for *shamed*)

"And they soon felt a new and delicious pleasure
which none but the bitterly disappointed can feel."
"What is that? What is that?"

Do not say diff-cult-y
Do not say joy-f'ly

Do not say va-r'a-ble
Not complaince for complaints
Not duss, not en

from Walt Whitman's

CROSSING BROOKLYN FERRY

We understand, then, do we not?
What I promis'd without mentioning it, have you not accepted?
What the study could not teach—what the preaching could not
    accomplish, is accomplish'd, is it not?
What the push of reading could not start, is started by me per-
    sonally, is it not?

from Jonathan Edwards

DOCTRINE OF ORIGINAL SIN

It will follow from what has been observed, that God's upholding created substance, or causing existence in each successive moment, is altogether equivalent to an *immediate production out of nothing*, at each moment. Because its existence at this moment is not merely in part from *God*, but wholly from Him, and not in any part or degree, from its *antecedent existence*. God produces the effect as much from *nothing*, as if there had been nothing *before*. So that this effect differs not at all from the first creation, but only *circumstantially*.

Now, in the next place, let us see how the *consequence* of these things is to my present purpose. If the existence of created *substance*, in each successive moment, be wholly the effect of God's immediate power, in *that* moment, without any dependence on prior existence, as much as the first creation out of *nothing*, then what exists at this moment, by this power, is a *new effect*, and simply and absolutely considered, not the same with any past existence, though it be like it, and follows it according to a certain established method.* And there is no identity or oneness in the case, but

---

*When I suppose that an effect which is produced every moment, by a new action or exertion of power, must be a *new* effect in each moment, and not absolutely and numerically the same with that which existed in preceding moments, the thing that I intend may be illustrated by this example. The lucid color or brightness of the *moon*, as we look steadfastly upon it, seems to be a *permanent* thing, as though it were perfectly the same brightness continued. But indeed it is an effect produced every moment. It ceases, and is renewed, in each successive point of time; and so becomes altogether a *new* effect: at each instant; and no one thing that belongs to it is numerically the same that existed in the preceding moment. The rays of the sun, impressed on that body, and reflected from it, which cause the effect, are none of them the same. The impression, made in each moment on our sensory, is by the stroke of *new* rays; and the sensation, excited by the stroke, is a new effect, an effect of a *new* impulse. Therefore the brightness or lucid whiteness of this body is no more numerically the same thing with that which existed in the preceding moment, than the *sound* of the wind that blows now, is individually the same with the sound of the wind that blew just before, which, though it be like it, is not the same, any more than the agitated *air*, that makes the sound,

what depends on the *arbitrary* constitution of the Creator; who by his wise sovereign establishment so unites the successive new effects, that he *treats them as one*, by communicating to them like properties, relations, and circumstances; and so leads *us* to regard and treat them as *one*. When I call this an *arbitrary constitution*, I mean, it is a constitution which depends on nothing but the *divine will*; which divine will depends on nothing but the *divine wisdom*. In this sense, the whole *course of nature*, with all that belongs to it, all its laws and methods, and constancy and regularity, continuance and proceeding, is an *arbitrary constitution*. In this sense, the continuance of the very being of the world and all its parts, as well as the

is the same; or than the *water*, flowing in a river, that now passes by, is individually the same with that which passed a little before. And if it be thus with the brightness or color of the moon, so it must be with its *solidity*, and every thing else belonging to its substance, if all be, each moment, as much the immediate effect of a *new* exertion or application of power.

The matter may perhaps be in some respects still more clearly illustrated by this. The *images* of things in a *glass*, as we keep our eye upon them seem to remain precisely the same, with a continuing, perfect identity. But it is known otherwise. Philosophers well know that these images are constantly *renewed*, by the impression and reflection of *new* rays of light; so that the image impressed by the former rays is constantly vanishing, and a *new* image impressed by *new* rays every moment, both on the glass and on the eye. The image constantly renewed, by new successive rays, is no more numerically the same, than if it were by some artist put on anew with a pencil, and the colors constantly vanishing as fast as put on.

And truly so the matter must be with the *bodies* themselves, as well as their images. They also cannot be the same, with an absolute identity, but must be wholly renewed every moment, if the case be as has been proved, that their present existence is not, strictly speaking, at all the effect of their past existence; but is wholly every instant, the effect of a new agency, or exertion of power, of the cause of their existence. If so, the existence caused is every instant a new effect, whether the cause be *light*, or immediate *divine power*, or whatever it be . . .

manner of continued being, depends entirely on an *arbitrary constitution*. For it does not at all necessarily follow, that because there was sound, or light, or color, or resistance, or gravity, or thought, or consciousness, or any other dependent thing the last moment, that therefore there shall be the like at the next.

THE BREAK OF DAY

1

Looked for him
everywhere. Him
gone. Maybe never
having been
here? Couldn't re-
call. Looking.
The day out of
order. Urgent.
A dizziness inside me
like a length of
cloth, unfolding, and me
wanting to go round &
round that way, un-
folding, maybe
connected to something at
the end (maybe) un-
spooling, me riding
it down yet looking
for him, the *looking* an
unfolding (inward or is it
downward) and yet
after a while
there is nothing you're
looking for, nothing. So,
looking for him, yes,
but in order to
take part further in
this unfolding
which is a falling
inward, a not-

2

And now, I said, behold
human beings living
in an underground den
which has a mouth
towards the light
so they can only
see before them,
prevented by the chain
from turning round—
above and behind them a
fire blazing at a
distance, and between
the fire and prisoners
a raised way and
(you will see if you look)
a low wall, like a
screen—*I*
see—And you see, I said,
men passing
along the wall
carrying all sorts of statues
and figures of wood
which appear then
over the wall,
some of them talking,
others silent—
You have shown me
a strange image, these are
strange prisoners—like
ourselves, I

finding you can
ride the inward
suck of—Even with
an eye on you,
friend, reader, even
with a mirror on
the wall, or spaces
round, fixed,
someone talking,
a length of wire on
the table, even then
all the time this

replied, they see only
their own shadows
or the shadows of
one another which the fire
is throwing
on the opposite wall—*true,
true*—and of the objects
being carried they also
see only the shadow—*Yes*—
And if they were able to
converse with one another
would they not suppose

3

Shh . . .
       Close your eyes. Close them.
It's not even dawn yet, it's late.
Close them . . .
       And there is the fabric, mended now—
grainy, slick—

4

She did not under-
stand, he insisted.
He would send her
a black barège, twelve
yards, just enough
to make a dress.
The one you've on is
good enough for the home,

but you want another
for calls. I saw that
the very moment I
came in. I've a quick eye
for these things.
She faced him,
leaning against the wall.
The moon shone through
the open blinds.
At times the shadows
of the willows
hid her completely, then
she reappeared
suddenly. Leon,
on the floor beside her,
found under his hand
a ribbon—scarlet silk.
On the strength of it
she bought a length of
yellow madras with
large stripes. Lheureux
had recommended it.
A particularly
good buy. She dreamt
of getting a carpet and Lheureux
politely took to
supplying her with one.
She could no longer do
without his services.
Twenty times a day
she sent for him.
He at once interrupted

whatever he was doing.
This was in the early part of

                          5

. . . .then open them again—no light—no—something

powdery yet slick—the

continuum?—no luminosity and yet a sheen on it

which you could say is your listening

sprinkling over the green dark,

but not materially, no, a dust

                          6

But even when the
hair and nails
have been safely
cut, there remains
the difficulty of
disposing of them.
For a man may
be bewitched
by means
of the clippings of
his hair, the parings of
his nails, or any
other severed portion

of his person.
The sorcerer
takes some of the hair, spittle
or other body refuse
of the man he
wishes to injure,
wraps it in a leaf,
places the packet
in a bag woven
of threads
knotted in an intricate
manner then buried
with certain rites,
and thereupon the victim
wastes away
of a languishing sickness
which lasts
twenty days.
His life, however,
may be saved
by discovering and digging up
the buried hair or spittle.
As soon as this
is done, the power
of the charm
ceases. The Huzuls imagine
if mice get a person's
shorn hair
and make a nest of it
the person will suffer from
headache or become

. . . no luminosity and yet a sheen
which you could say is your listening
sprinkling over the green dark—
but not materially—no—a dust of

expectation.
Stay with me.
Can we make this a *thinking*, here, this determination
between us to co-

exist. No nail on the wall yet. No cry in the dawn.
No dawn.
No green as yet, no bloom of
paths and possibilities—arcades, archways—no maze, no . . .

8

And suppose further
that the prisoners
heard an echo which came
from the other side,
would they not be sure
that the voice they heard
came from the passing
shadow? *No question—*
—To them, I said,
truth would be literally
nothing but the shadows
of the images—*that
is certain*—and now

9

It oftened seemed to Leon
that his soul
fleeing towards her
broke like a wave
against the contours of her
and was drawn irresistibly
down into the whiteness.
She would take his head suddenly
between her hands
and kiss him quickly on
the forehead crying
Adieu and rush down
the stairs. Night

look again,
see what will follow
if the prisoner
were released and
disabused—
Compelled suddenly
to stand up
and turn round
and look towards
the light, he
will suffer sharp pain,
the glare will distress him,
his instructor
pointing to the objects
as they pass (that burn him)
and requiring him to
name them—Will he not
fancy that the shadows
he formerly saw
are truer than the objects
which now are shown him?
Will he not have
pain in his eyes?—*Yes, yes*—

would be falling.
You seem so strange this
evening he would
say. Oh it's
nothing, nothing Emma
would reply. Oh! don't
move, don't speak! Look
at me. He knelt
on the ground before her.
Resting his elbows on
her lap. Murmuring.
Then he drew from
his pocket a list
of goods not
paid for: to wit, the
curtains, the carpet, the
material for the arm
chair, several dresses and diverse
articles of dress.
But if you haven't ready money
you've some
property. And he re-
called for her attention
a miserable little shack
situated at Barneville, near
Annale, which brought in

10

Then open them again—No light—not

yet—Something powdery yet slick—the

continuum?—no luminosity and yet a sheen in it (on it?)
which you could say is my listening
sprinkling over the green dark—
but not materially—a dust of

expectation.
Stay with me.
Can we make this a *thinking*, here, this determination
between us to co-

exist. No nail in the wall yet. No cry in the dawn.
No dawn.
No green as yet, no bloom of
paths and possibilities—arcades, archways—no maze, no underneaths.

How shall we face in this? (We shall not)
And all the memories of *things* bothering awake now. (They
                                          shall not).
And *summer Sundays in the Park*—where shall they go and hum

and stay, the gauze of that low-key history wrapped round and
                                          round,
the nail at the heart (shall not),
all you can't say anymore
unwrapping—flapping off—that nail in its wall—unravelling.
Where is that other land. We have grown weary . . . A field of lights.

The whole cannot exist without the parts.

Stay, stay.

11

Then in the dark a sound—a *whereabout*—
like a ridged place in the low whine,
boring an opening—birdsong: 2 notes—
sounds like *flatbed*; sounds like *abject*; like

mudflat   turn back—

making a pandemonium of the stillness now, 2 notes clotting the
                                 dark up into them,
making rafters in that dark, co-

ordinates (*show dad*) spiralings
(*know that*) of dark so that it's suddenly a thing of

offsprung bits, rungs of dark within the rungs of
listening and then it's a
place, a *fate*, long distance poking tiny holes in,
and hoarfrost (four other notes now) (answering),

and limbs which won't whiten along with the rest so
        they're trees, and in them
leaves that won't stay put so they're a
flock, prickling the silences, chatter, song—
the flock of my listenings now flat-out
        one on one
with the flock that's

12

And why are there
essents rather

than nothing?
Why is there
anything at
all? That is
the question and
perhaps it
will strike but
once like a
muffled bell,
gradually
dying away, but then
everything seems
endlessly common-
place—for consider
the earth
within the
endless darkness of
space in the
universe—by
way of comparison
it is a grain of
sand—between
it and the next
grain there extends
a mile or more of
emptiness—and on the
surface of this
grain lives
a crawling be-
wildered swarm of
supposedly in-
telligent animals
who for a

moment have
discovered knowl-
edge: in
relation to the
essent as
such in its
entirety the
asking of the question
is not just any

13

And also, also, it is plain
that commodities
cannot go to market
and make exchange
of their own accord—
that we must therefore
have recourse to
their guardians who are
also their owners—
that commodities are without
power of resistance
against man—that if
they are wanting in
docility, he
can use force, he
can *take possession*
of them—let us look
at the matter
a little closer—
for a commodity appears

at first sight
a very trivial thing
easily understood,
but it is, in reality,
a very queer thing,
abounding in meta-
physical subtleties,
theological niceties—you see,

14

It's that the dark seems to be *composed*.
Although it's featureless as I look up with mine.
Purr.
Has voice in it. A lyre? A concealed

weapon?

As if there's something in it for safekeeping, something
                                        of which I
am the paraphrase

as if lifts up above me now, a'labyrinth of variegated darks—

or is it *one* dark?—

a momentum without motion or direction
and in it
like a pronged cry or a tuning fork
this body of which I

am the core, looking up, tamping the dark with
                                my looking up,

or is it *airing up*—I cannot tell—
into this mob of suitors, cherubs, gypsies, sophists—

not really hallowed because so crowded,

but free—yes that—the ultimate orchard of

voices, thronging, one added every second, here's the plastic
surgeon now, the airline agent, the mistress of the small-time
Sardinian industrialist whose idea it really was to sell
the Costa Smeralda,

and the one whose jewels
no-one will ever find,
the one whose jewels the planet will burn up at the end
containing.
                    You see, there are NO MISTAKES   BUT

there is this passage-through where the notion of error

APPLIES and I (Adam?) must consider,

that if the dark lifts away from me in this way, a tautology for
what is trapped in this sealed skin of mine (INSIDE),
then what am I to
                    want?
What is it cannot be judged?
What is it
            is corporeal but still concealed?

Does not involve error?
Perfectly hollow?

I feel my footnote evaporating.
I feel the skin tighten like Saran Wrap now, the god finishing up

the form—privacies are added—the starry dizziness
    rammed into the eyepits—deep in—

the symmetry like a forked shriek effected—two and then
                                    two—His thumbs
smoothing it out—
and Balance struck through the top of me—down through—
steel rod—slicing the parts of the visible forever from—

severing the front from that parched earth behind me now—
cramping me in,
the sill of nothing to nothing,
this orphaned forwardness now swelling up, starched—a cancellation but
                                        of what I

can't say—and mended (*whoosh*)
muddled—(what *want?*)—

15

So that I know the morning dove, I hear it.
First right beside, then
further away—4 holes in the listening—

a sort-of-full but really empty sound—

now with a yellow forearm—very long—of sun through it

which will spread of course and get tired of pointing

each thing out as if there were hardly enough time—

Until it is all this pointing and indicating, crisscrossing of fire—
                         warp and woof of urgent illuminations—
see this? now this? hurry, look, don't miss this, friend—

                   (I will not be called friend)—

and this black spot over there—it's for your own good—

and over there the hedgerows which show how answers come—

and then the cliffs now—right up to them—

and then a flish of crows through the foreground like a cough,

recalling me (so that this crazy back and forth begins),

the main point having changed,

here wear these clothes, friend, *friend*,

all the lackeys of the light rushing in, the minor attendants

bringing in new props taking them away

so that you feel the plot—or something like it, *minutes*—begin,

a bit dusty now as the sun is *equally dis-*

tributed over all

and you realize

that we are *in a drama*—and then the camera starts

rolling—so silently—almost soundlessly—although if you
                                                    listen,

deep into it now, past the other sounds, past the
                        listening, if you listen . . . ?

16

Oh but tell me, morning dust, dust of the green in things, *on* things, dust of water

   whirling up off the matter, mist, hoarfrost, dust over the

fiddlehead, what am I
      supposed

to take, what?

17

(He put it into Emma's hand)

Shutting the great temple gate,
Creak! it goes:
An autumn evening.

Nobody there;
A child asleep
In the mosquito net.

Two houses!
Two houses making rice-cakes:
Autumn rain.

The autumn wind is blowing;
We are alive and can see each other.
You and I.

The owner of the field
Goes to see how the scarecrow is,
And comes back.

The autumn wind
Moved the scarecrow
And passed on.

A sound of something:
The scarecrow
Has fallen down of itself.

Yes! Yes! I cried,
But someone still knocked
On the snow-mantled gate.

from THE NOTEBOOKS *of Leonardo da Vinci*

OF MOVEMENT AND WEIGHT

1

In equal movements made in equal time the mover will always have more power than the thing which is moved. And the mover will be so much the more powerful than the thing moved in proportion as the movement of this thing moved exceeds the length of movement of its mover; and the difference of the power of the mover over that of the thing moved will be so much less in proportion as the length of the movement made by the thing moved is less than the movement of this mover.

2

I find that force is infinite together with time; and that weight is finite together with the weight of the whole globe of the terrestrial machine.

I find that the stroke of indivisible time is movement, and that this movement is of many varieties, namely natural, accidental and participating; and this participating movement achieves its greatest power when it changes from the accidental to the natural, that is in the middle of its course; and the natural is more powerful at the end than in any other place; the accidental is strongest in the third and weakest at the close.

3

Weight, force, a blow and impetus are the children of movement because they are born from it.

Weight and force always desire their death, and each is maintained by violence.

Impetus is frequently the reason why movement prolongs the desire of the thing moved.

4

Gravity and levity are accidental powers which are produced by one element being drawn through, or driven into, another.

INVENTION OF THE OTHER

1

When the music ended she noticed the light.
The music has ended it said all over the things.
    It moved under the white narcissus
blooms, splaying-up and varnishing the green flutings
    beneath. She watched.
There was nothing
    it didn't leave behind
in the ending

    of the music
which seemed to linger for a time in these gentlest lickings
    of morning-light—as if they, more even than her, wanted
to see what they touched—
    as if the music had finally ended for that
purpose—that the light be allowed
    this

    interval—not silence, not even free of
echoes (the music still ripe in the silence after all: the light now
    the heels of the music, its
offing, little yelps in the way it slavers the panes,
    indiscriminate though utterly attentive) . . .

    Until the mind watching the light
lift the edges of the pillow up—
    (the weave revealed, the stain in the brocade, the thinning
                    of the fabric
at the seam)—watching it lift
    then put each thing *back down*—(whatever it was looking for

not there, not there)—until the mind,
watching, became itself the heels of that
       light, its outermost edges, congeries of small thinkings, little
                                                          whelps,
desire: utterly unequivocal yet
       utterly without

       knowledge, a long licking across the surface of
matter . . . And the body, the gravity from whence this whole thing
       rose—(*the body!* she thought, as if she had forgotten it)—the body
                                                                    itself
the offspring of this long thin waiting laying itself down as
       an act of
looking—And all of it (the heels of the music's having ended, the
       end of the music, the end of the music's

       ending) now changes rung upon a listening that still
listened, is listening, as the last note carries the air in it and is
       carried by
that air, dusty, in which the light, and the molecules of watching, and
                                                          the motes of
       listening, are changes rung, rung, but upon what—adamant—quick—
                                                                    upon
what?

                                        2

       She went to the windowpane. Sun went behind clouds.
Returned.
       She stood there in the changes, the vast, escalloped

feathery endings
       slipping over her then off
in smoky veils, ash-yellow rufflings, wisps, licks—lifting

off—each cloud-shadow erasing
the shadow of and the shadow of . . .

She watched the row of bushes, the greens in them, the swaying green.

OPULENCE

The self-brewing of the amaryllis rising before me.
Weeks of something's decomposing—like hearsay
growing—into this stringent self-analysis—
a tyranny of utter self-reflexiveness—
its nearness to the invisible a deep fissure
the days suck round as its frontiers trill, slur
—a settling-ever-upward and then,
                                    now,
this utterly sound-free-though-tongued opening
where some immortal scale is screeched—
bits of *clench, jolt, fray* and *assuage*—
bits of *gnaw* and *pulse* and, even, *ruse*
—impregnable dribble—wingbeat at a speed
too slow to see—stepping out of the casing outstretched,
                                    high-heeled—
something from underneath coaxing the packed buds up,
loosening their perfect fit—the smooth skin between them
                                    striating then
beginning to wrinkle and fold
so as to loosen the tight dictation of the four inseparable polished
                                    and bullioned
buds—color seeping up till the icy green releases the sensation of
                                    a set of reds
imprisoned in it, flushed, though not yet truly
visible—the green still starchy—clean—
till the four knots grow loose in their armor,
and the two dimensions of their perfect-fit fill out and a third,
                                    shadow, seeps in
loosening and loosening,
and the envelope rips,
and the fringes slip off and begin to fray at their newly freed tips,
and the enameled, vaulting, perfectly braided
                    Immaculate

is jostled, unpacked—
the force, the phantom, now sending armloads up
into the exclamation,
and the skin marbles, and then, when I look again,
has already begun to speckle, then blush, then a solid un-
avoidable incarnadine,
the fourness of it now maneuvering, vitalized,
like antennae rearranging constantly,
the monologue reduced—or is it expanded—to
this chatter seeking all the bits of light,
the four of them craning this way then that according to
                                              the time
of day, the drying wrinkled skirts of the casing
now folded-down beneath, formulaic,
the light wide-awake around it—or is it the eye—
yes yes yes yes says the mechanism of the underneath tick tock—
and no footprints to or from the place—
no footprints to or from—

Green netting set forth;
spectrum of greens a bird arcs through; low and
                                   perfect
postponement.
The wind moves the new leaves aside—as if there were
                                   an inventory
taken—till they each wink the bit of light
they're raised into—full greenish-yellow of
                       newly-born leaf
flickering then for an instant incandescent with full
                             sun—
outline of green so bright it
            seems
to scorch-open the surround—ripped, fingery serration
diagramming in barbarous brillance the juncture of
                       presence to
absence—although there are sandbars—and waves breaking where
                                     the wind
tufts, twists, slapping itself up through these matters it can't
                              get through
—thrashing round and in them—or is it them dissipating
                       abundance
by not holding-on to any of this wind's
fortitude—no record kept of the progress—no
invasion which is not let through, let pass . . .
—Dear history of this visible world, scuffling
                 at the edges of you is
no edge, no whereabout—wind and leaf and postponement
and fact and fragrance—where is your inventory of
events? what plank, what underneath to fortify?—are you not
                               also an
exemplification?—I watch the invasion this morning

again and again—airshafts seizing my young maples from
                                        underneath,
making the undersides of leaves *aluminum,*
wrinkling the shadowplay and the seeming till I feel
                              something I'd call
indecision, but, but . . . Reader, do you taste
                        salt now if
I say to you the air is *salt*—that there is iodine from fresh
after-rain ozone rising in wafts between me and this
                        illustration . . . Reader,
wind blowing through these lines I wish were branches,
searchlight in daylight, trying as I
                  am trying
to find a filament of the real like some twist of handwriting glowing
                                                in the middle
distance—somewhere up here, in the air—can we,
                                    together,
(if I say salt, if I say fresh-cut grass, late April, the sound of
                                    sprinkler on
some distance away but still within
staining-range of the sinking whisperings of this gentle
                                    wind,
and a hammer now, one car sputtering down)—can we,
                              together,
make a listening here, like a wick sunk deep in this mid-
                                    temperate
morning-light, can we make its tip—your reading my
                        words—burn, you
in some other time than this, maybe under an arc lamp
                              tonight?
holding currency in one hand? stepping off some curb or
                              orderly zone?—

—some lodging?—what race of people were your people?—does
your hair
bristle in cold—can you remember *marionettes* or is this
a word you've never used—can you look it up
wherever you are—
have you seen corpses—have you perjured yourself and are there
laws there now
regarding reference—and the pastures of syntax, what have they
produced? Oh
spring wind . . . I watch the edges of everything you fret and
scribble. Is there an argument in all this turning and turning?
Is it towards presence—as it seems? Is it turning an *absence*
towards us,
giving it face? And you, green face—mournful, tormented, self-
swallowing, graven,
navel-and-theory face, what is it you turn towards, green history-
face,
what is your migration from?

I dig my hands into the absolute. The surface
                              breaks
into shingled, grassed clusters; lifts.
If I press, pick-in with fingers, pluck,
I can unfold the loam. It is tender. It is a tender
maneuver, hands making and unmaking promises.
Diggers, forgetters. . . . A series of successive single instances . . .
Frames of reference moving . . .
The speed of light, down here, upthrown, in my hands:
bacteria, milky roots, pilgrimages of spores, deranged
                              and rippling
mosses. What heat is this in me
that would *thaw time*, making bits of instance
                              overlap
shovel by shovelful—my present a wind blowing through
                              this culture
slogged and clutched-firm with decisions, over-ridings,
                              opportunities
taken? . . . If I look carefully, there in my hand, if I
                    break it apart without
crumbling: husks, mossy beginnings and endings, ruffled
                              airy loambits,
and the greasy silks of clay crushing the pinerot
                              in . . .
Erasure. Tell me something and then take it back.
Bring this pellucid moment—here on this page now
                    as on this patch
of soil, my property—bring it up to the top and out
                                   of
sequence. Make it dumb again—won't you?—what
                              would it
take? Leach the humidities out, the things that will
                              insist on

making meaning. Parch it. It isn't hard: just take this
                                        shovelful
and spread it out, deranged, a vertigo of single
                                clots
in full sun and you can, easy, decivilize it, un-
                        hinge it
from its plot. Upthrown like this, I think you can
                        eventually
abstract it. Do you wish to?
Disentangled, it grows very very clear.
Even the mud, the sticky lemon-colored clay
hardens and then yields, crumbs.
I can't say what it is then, but the golden-headed
                        hallucination,
mating, forgetting, speckling, inter-
                locking,
will begin to be gone from it and then its glamorous
                                veil of
echoes and muddy nostalgias will
be gone. If I touch the slender new rootings they show me
                        how large I
am, look at these fingers—what a pilot—I touch, I press
                        their slowest
electricity. . . . What speed is it at?
What speed am I at here, on my knees, as the sun traverses now
                        and just begins
to touch my back. What speed where my fingers, under the
                        dark oaks,
are suddenly touched, lit up—so white as they move, the ray for
                        a moment
on them alone in the small wood.

White hands in the black-green glade,
opening the muddy cartoon of the present, taking the tiny roots
                                        of the moss
apart, hired hands, curiosity's small army, so white
                        in these greens—
make your revolution in the invisible temple,
make your temple in the invisible
revolution—I can't see the errands you run, hands gleaming
                        for this instant longer
like tinfoil at the bottom here of the tall
                        whispering oaks . . .
Listen, Boccioni the futurist says a galloping horse
                        has not four
legs (it has twenty)—and "at C there is no sequence
because there is no time"—and since
at lightspeed, etc. (everything is simultaneous): my hands
serrated with desires, shoved into these excavated
                                        fates
—mauve, maroons, gutters of flecking golds—
my hands are living in myriad manifestations
                        of light. . . .
"All forms of imitation are to be despised."
"All subjects previously used must be discarded."
"At last we shall rush rapidly past objectiveness" . . .
Oh enslavement will you take these hands
                        and hold them in
for a time longer? Tops of the oaks, do you see my tiny
                        golden hands
pushed, up to the wrists,
into the present? Star I can't see in daylight, young, light
                        and airy star—
I put the seed in. The beam moves on.

And how shall this soliloquy reverberate
over the hillside? Who shall be
the singleness over the yawning speckled lambency?
I think I feel my thinking-self and how it
stands—its condensation, its voice-track like an
electric backbone up
into the meadow's shadow-play, up like a prophet of utterly non-
deciduous tongue who chatters on while the buds and shadows
scatter. Who shall the listening be?
A huntress ran across, near dusk—we saw the quiver
like a small gleam on the back of a mossy knoll or maybe
water between the far trees.
An alphabet flew over, made liquid syntax for a while,
diving and rising, forking, a caprice of clear meanings,
right pauses, unwrapping the watching-temptation—
then chopped and scattered, one last one chittering away,
then silence, then the individual screeches of the nighthunters
at dusk, the hollows sucked in around that cry.

THE SURFACE

It has a hole in it. Not only where I
                    concentrate.
The river still ribboning, twisting up,
                    into its re-
arrangements, chill enlightenments, tight-knotted
                                    quickenings
and loosenings—whispered messages dissolving
                              the messengers—
the river still glinting-up into its handfuls, heapings,
                                    glassy
forgettings under the river of
my attention—
and the river of my attention laying itself down—
                                    bending,
reassembling—over the quick leaving-offs and windy
                                    obstacles—
and the surface rippling under the wind's attention—
rippling over the accumulations, the slowed-down drifting
                                    permanences
of the cold
bed.
I say *iridescent* and I look down.
The leaves very still as they are carried.

NOTES

All passages referred to as "adaptations" are edited, rewritten in spots, or assembled out of fragments collected from the larger work named. This also applies, in small measure, to the epigraphs.

"A CAPPELLA": Section 5: These are the dying Socrates' final words.

"STEERING WHEEL": The passage in quotes is from an essay by the poet Jeffrey Hamilton on George Oppen.

"CONCERNING THE RIGHT TO LIFE" and "THE DREAM OF THE UNIFIED FIELD": The passages which make up the final gestures of the poems are rewritten sections from the *Diario of Christopher Columbus, First Voyage to America, 1492–93*, abstracted by Fray Bartolome de La Casas (translated by Oliver Dunn and James E. Kelley Jr.).

"RELATIVITY: A QUARTET": Section 3 was set in motion by Harold Bloom's *The Book of J*. Section 3 also quotes three zen "sayings" from *The Transmission of Light* by Zen Master Keizan, translated by Thomas Cleary.

"ON DESCRIPTION": The material is from *Illuminations* and from the first draft of a letter dated *Ibiza, August 13, 1933* and quoted by Gershom Scholem in his essay, "Walter Benjamin and His Angel."

"EVENT HORIZON": The two lines quoted from the poetry of Bei-Dao are unaltered.

"NOTES ON THE REALITY OF THE SELF": Some of the phrasing is culled from Constantin Stanislavsky's *Building a Character*, translated by Elizabeth Reynolds Hapgood.

"*From Brecht's* A SHORT ORGANUM FOR THE THEATRE": This collage uses John Willett's translation from *Brecht: On Theatre* (Hill & Wang).

"ANNUNCIATION WITH A BULLET IN IT": The epigraph is from Wallace Stevens. Parts 5 through 12, and 17, are composed of quotations (sometimes edited or slightly altered in their syntax) collected from the Holocaust diary, *Fragments of Isabella, A Memoir of Auschwitz*, by Isabella Leitner, originally published by Bantam Dell, now out of print. Section 13 contains a few phrases from Lyotard's *Le Differand*.

"ON DESIRE": This is a slightly edited excerpt from *Language, Thought, and Reality*, a collection of essays by Benjamin Whorf and John Carroll, published by MIT Press. This material is culled from the chapter titled "An American Indian Model of the Universe."

"From McGuffey's NEW FIFTH READER": This is a collage composed of fragments from the 1857 edition.

"THE BREAK OF DAY": This contains some passages, slightly edited or rewritten, from Plato (2 and 8), Flaubert's *Madame Bovary* (4, 9), Sir James Frazer's *The Golden Bough* (6), Heidegger's *Introduction to Metaphysics* (12), and Karl Marx's *Capital* (13). The poem was initially composed (under the title "MATERIALISM") to accompany a series of paintings by Stephen Schultz.

"NOTES ON THE REALITY OF THE SELF": The haiku that compose this poem are by Shiki, Issa, Buson, and Kyorai.

"From the NOTEBOOKS of Leonardo da Vinci": The collection is arranged and rendered into English by Edward MacCurdy (London: Jonathan Cape).

"MANIFEST DESTINY": This poem is for Diana Michener, whose sequence of photos on Leda and the Swan helped frame and focus the second section.

Thanks to Connie Greenleaf for being the gardener and neighbor of "Concerning the Right to Life" and "Subjectivity."